HEAVEN'S DYNASTY

How The Kingdom
Is Being Restored
Father Through Son

BY
CHRISTOPHER MONAGHAN

acknowledgements

I dedicate this work to my wife, Debbie, who has always stood by my side, selflessly co-pioneering the work of the kingdom. Her willingness to be a radical and engage the heart of God inspires me and so many others- all this while faithfully serving as my wife and a mother of five. This book would not exist without her enthusiastic sacrifice.

Special thanks to Karl Baird, John and Gayla Meredith, Sarah Chasteen and Tricia Meredith for their countless hours of editing and input as this book was coming together. Thank you for keeping me grounded in love.

c o n t e n t s

introduction

*H*eaven's Dynasty is a book about something very simple and obvious. Even though theology and theory have been a great passion of mine for many years, I have discovered that people are what really matter. If people don't understand the theology, we may be looking at the kingdom of God from the wrong perspective. Searching through complex theological concepts without a heart of simplicity, disconnects the heart and mind, often causing us to forfeit the point of our seeking. Knowing God and His Son Jesus is the focus.

What you are about to read has been a journey for me, one that I can relate through the following analogy. It is a story that took place on the border of two nations that were hostile towards one another. Everyday a man came to the border with two buckets full of sand to cross over into the other country. Day after day, the guard searched suspiciously through the sand and when finding nothing, reluctantly let him cross. This same event took place daily for twenty-five years until the day when the countries united and the border patrol was no longer needed. On that final day, as he was coming back across the border the suspicious guard questioned him, "You were a smuggler! I know you were! What were you smuggling?" To the guards surprise, the man commented, "Buckets."

I have often felt very much like the border patrol guard who missed the obvious. Heaven's Dynasty is my attempt to reveal a truth simply presented in the Scriptures. I do not have some brand new revelation to disclose to you. The concept of the kingdom of God flowing as a dynasty is weaved throughout the Bible from beginning to end!

Heaven's Dynasty could be summed up in one powerful thought: "generational relationship." More specifically, this is a book about the very unique and special relationship between God the Father, and His only Son, Jesus Christ. This interaction between the Father and Son molds our view of the kingdom of God and how it operates in our lives.

Peter writes explicitly to believers as he nears the end of his life saying, **"I will make every effort to see that after my departure you will always be able to remember these things."** (2 Peter 1:15) "These things" Peter points to, refer to the very intimate and incredible moment between the Father and Son as written in the next two verses:

We did not follow cleverly invented stories when we told you about the power and coming of our Lord Jesus Christ, but we were eyewitnesses of his majesty. For he received honor and glory from God the Father when the voice came to him from the Majestic Glory, saying, "This is my Son, whom I love; with him I am well pleased." (2 Peter 1:16-17)

A powerful exchange took place at that very moment! The Father openly declared His love and pleasure for His Son. And in exchange, the Son received honor and glory from His Father. It was the Father's joy to bestow this honor upon His Son. Everything He had, He gladly gave His Son, with whom He was 'well pleased.'

Christianity is not a system of ideas we think about or list of rules we attempt to follow. Christianity is an encounter with the love of God and the forgiveness of Jesus: an encounter that has penetrated our hearts and wrecked our lives. God made His plan known to us by sending His Son and Jesus' mission was to make the Father known to the world!

All of us understand the concepts of parent, child and family structures, because we all experience them. We understand on intimate levels what it is to be a son, a daughter, or a parent. All of us can relate to the great hunger within us to be loved by our fathers and mothers. We parents, as well, have an undying love for our children.

This is certainly not complicated theology. It is the very heart of God to show exactly who He is, and to reveal to us that no greater relationships exist. Not only are we granted the same privilege, to actually become sons and daughters of God, I also believe that the very patterns established in heaven, are soon to be released in greater measure on the earth.

In this writing I will touch upon the first major conflict in the Christian realm that sparked great controversy. I will address the concept of the Trinity, the most common model that Christians have been taught in their understanding of God. The interaction between God the Father, Jesus Christ, and the Holy Spirit does not need to be mysterious. The trademark message of the Trinity has been confusion not simplicity. Those who have gone before us may have complicated our minds by introducing concepts and words to our theology that were not wrong per se, just unnecessary.

This book is my attempt at providing a framework in our thinking about the kingdom that will ground our message in the core understanding of God as Father and Jesus as Son. This writing will take us back to the original teachings of the New Testament. Jesus is the Son who will continue His Father's dynasty. He will rule until the kingdom of God is established on earth. This dynasty is the very kingdom we continue to advance in the name of Jesus.

I have been greatly blessed as the father of four sons. If I owned a factory, and one day turned over the entire operation to one of them, I would fully expect the employees to respond to their authority with the same respect and honor that they had shown me. I would not allow any employee to bypass the authority of my son and come directly to me, because the factory now belongs to the son I have chosen to run the company.

In the same way, Father God conferred the Kingdom upon His Son. No one can bypass the Son to the Father, because an irrevocable transference has occurred. All of God's authority has been granted to His Son. This very exchange speaks of the greatness of our God. He completely trusts His Son to rule and reign with all power and might.

Jesus is our example of one who is receiving the kingdom. Remember the parable of the tenants:

A man planted a vineyard, rented it to some farmers and went away for a long time. At harvest time he sent a servant to the tenants so they would give him some of the fruit of the vineyard. But the tenants beat him and sent

him away empty-handed. He sent another servant, but that one also they beat and treated shamefully and sent away empty-handed. He sent still a third, and they wounded him and threw him out. Then the owner of the vineyard said, "What shall I do? I will send my son, whom I love; perhaps they will respect him." But when the tenants saw him, they talked the matter over. "This is the heir," they said. "Let's kill him, and the inheritance will be ours." So they threw him out of the vineyard and killed him. (Luke 20:9-14)

In this parable, Jesus is clearly the son of the vineyard owner. The tenants recognized him as the rightful heir and realize that without the son in the picture, they could claim the inheritance. The heir is destined to receive power and authority from the Father and this parable foretold what was about to take place in the life of Jesus.

This parable teaches us that God, as a Father, is seeking to release His inheritance to His Son. And then a most amazing truth emerges: Jesus then willingly releases this very power to us, His church, through His death and resurrection! He desires that we share in His inheritance. This is good news!

The Father and Son rule together on the throne, yet now the Son rules in heaven and on earth until all things are restored. Our charge is to follow in His footsteps. Friends, we will not be playing harps and sitting on clouds in the sweet by and by. We are destined to sit on His throne as well. "To him who overcomes, I will give the right to sit with me on my throne, just as I overcame and sat down with my Father on his throne." (Revelation 3:21)

I suggest you meditate on that idea for a moment. What an amazing inheritance we share with Him! This one scripture alone gives us the undeniable promise that because of Jesus, we too have the right to our Abba Father's lap.

Did you ever find comfort, strength, and power as you sat on your Daddy's lap? You are destined to sit there *with* Him, obtaining all that your heart has ever longed for. We must not forget that, **"God raised us up with Christ and seated us with him in the heavenly realms in Christ Jesus."** (Ephesians 2:6)

My desire is that this book will take you on a journey that simplifies your relationship with The Father through His Son. As a graduate of a Messianic Jewish Bible School, I have incorporated a Jewish understanding of the New Testament that is often lost in our Western minded theology. In my studies, I found that early theologians used many philosophical arguments instead of God's Word. I believe that in order to understand the greatest story ever told we must stick to the basic premises. God the Father is establishing a dynasty through His Son, Jesus. What are the implications of this? How have we strayed from this one basic truth?

This writing has allowed me to make the rule and reign of Jesus the centerpiece of my ministry. God's plan for salvation is irrefutably intertwined with His Son. The Lord Jesus is to be treated the same way we treat God Himself because He has ascended to the throne. The dynasty of God hinges upon the Son ruling in righteousness and justice. The kingdom of God is advancing *through* His Son and there is no other name under heaven by which man can be saved.

Many of us live with a democratic mindset instead of a kingdom mindset. A king in ancient times would establish his son upon his throne, thus beginning a new era throughout the kingdom. Jesus told His disciples, in anticipation of His inauguration, **"I tell you the truth, some who are standing here will not taste death before they see the kingdom of God come with power."** (Mark 9:1) Let's begin by examining the meaning of dynasty and how this concept applies to the kingdom of God.

Reflections

1. Peter made every effort to see that after his departure, the disciples remembered something very important! He pointed to the time when Jesus received honor and glory from God the Father. What does Peter want his disciples to never forget?

2. Have you been confused about the role Jesus has taken as the Son of God? How does the concept of dynasty fit into your model of walking with God?

3. Were you raised in a democracy? (i.e. voting for a candidate and the one with the majority of votes wins) How does the kingdom of God operate differently than a democracy?

chapter one
Dynasty Defined

A dynasty is a succession of persons belonging to the same family, who, through various means and forms maintain power, influence or authority over the course of generations.[1] A ruling territory or dynasty is often called an "era", which is used to describe the length of time in which a certain family reigned over a kingdom.

In modern day terminology, consider the following example. In 1988, George H. W. Bush was elected to become the 41st President of the United States. In 2000, George W. Bush Jr. became the 43rd President of the United States. The presidency

---

[1] "Dynasty - Metapedia." *Main Page - Metapedia.* Web. 20 Apr. 2011. <http://en.metapedia.org/wiki/Dynasty>.

is one office that a father and son ruled in separate time periods. This could be called the 'Bush era'.

Heaven's Dynasty is continued through the Son of God, Jesus. This era will continue through the kingdom of the Son until reconciliation and restoration occurs. Our attention now must be upon Jesus, who rules as the son of a King and as a King!

In the next few chapters, I want to discuss the main division that took place in the early church. Christian leaders struggled over the questions: "How could God be one when you have both the Father and Son?"

I want to present to you a Biblical and simple view of the Kingdom of God and our King. A good teacher will simplify the complicated. Often the most powerful truths are found in the simplest of statements.

Changing Operating Systems

In the computer market today, there are two main operating systems that are available: Mac and Windows PC. I recently purchased a Mac computer, even though I had been accustomed to Windows PC. Initially I was shocked, because I could not even perform some of the simplest of tasks! But the more I worked with the Mac, the more I discovered how natural it felt. I had to retrain myself and let go of my old ways and begin working a new system. The work paid off and now I have access to better software and more stability. All the programs I had used on my Windows PC were either useless, or had to be modified to work within my new operating system.

In the same way, I believe the early church switched operating systems within the first couple centuries of the early church. The language for the operating systems had to change, and so we use language that is often not even used in Scripture. This sparked a question in my heart, *"Why should we use language that neither Christ Himself or any of the New Testament writers used?"*

The operating system that must first change is our thought process. I recognize that change does not come easily. You may experience discomfort at first, but as we study together, my hope is that you will open up your mind to new ways of thinking. Early Jewish believers were born into a way of thinking that later followers of Jesus did not have. We must return to the "new wineskin" in preparation for the new wine.

And no one pours new wine into old wineskins. If he does, the wine will burst the skins, and both the wine and the wineskins will be ruined. No, he pours new wine into new wineskins. (Mark 2:22)

Much of what I will discuss in this book has come because of my involvement in the Messianic Jewish movement. I graduated from a Messianic Bible Institute based in Gaithersburg, Maryland in the 1990's. Most of my previous theological training seemed complicated and hard to grasp. Theology, from a Jewish perspective, was naturally explained, yet profound and powerful. This intrigued me.

As I began to teach truths from a Jewish perspective, I discovered most people were able to flow with the truth, *without stumbling into legalism or falling out of grace.* The New Testament must be read with the light of the Hebraic scriptures in the background. History reveals to us that this background was replaced with another source by the 3rd and 4th century after

11

Christ. The reasoning of man soon replaced simplicity of covenant faith as the backdrop of the teachings of the church.

Formal statements were also developed in the early church that began using the language of the new operating system. These statements are called 'Creeds'. Many of the early Creeds sought to enforce truth and bring unity, but because these statements were often empowered by the Roman sword, revival did not come to the church. The body of Christ and the world soon entered into 1,000 years of darkness. The Dark Ages ended with the spark of Martin Luther bringing back truths that had long been forgotten.

Could it be that the next Reformation will catapult us into 1,000 years of light-, which is called the Millennium? In this time period, Jesus Christ, the Son of God, will rule and reign here on earth, completing the work the Father sent Him to accomplish.

Dynasty and The Kingdom of God

The concept of Dynasty theology emphasizes this Father to Son transference of the kingdom of God. I submit this teaching to you, with prayer, hoping that you will discover the powerful revelation of our Heavenly Father, releasing His authority to His precious Son. As a result, the Son has been glorified and is *now* releasing His Spirit into you and me to assist us in bringing the kingdom of God to earth. The yearning for heaven to invade the natural realm is the cry of His people!

The Spirit and the bride say, "Come!" And let him who hears say, "Come!" Whoever is thirsty, let him come; and whoever wishes, let him take the free gift of the water of life. (Revelation 22:17)

Every dynasty has a significant transition period. Usually it is the death of the Father that releases the Son into His legacy. Yet in the kingdom of God, it was the death of the Son that actually elevated Him to the throne. A most unusual dynasty was birthed that day on Calvary.

The concept of Dynasty is often referred to in Scripture as 'the house of _____'. When King David desired to bless the son of his deceased covenant partner Jonathan, he asked, **"Is there anyone still left of the house of Saul to whom I can show kindness for Jonathan's sake?"** (2 Samuel 9:1). Notice that David did not refer to the "house of Jonathan" but rather the "house of Saul". Jonathan was actually part of Saul's dynasty. This same concept continues in the Kingdom of God. The personal name of God is Yahweh and Jesus is continuing "the house of Yahweh."

History tells us that many good and powerful dynasties have fallen because of corrupt sons. But a good son rules in the image and character of his father, ensuring that the throne will endure forever. And as the throne endures, so does the kingdom.

The Kingdom Inaugurated

The word *inaugurated* describes the beginning or introduction of a new policy or administration. The word describes the action of formally admitting someone to office or officially

13

opening a project or organization for public use.[2] The process of His inauguration is the event Jesus described to Peter, James and John:

And he said to them, "I tell you the truth, some who are standing here will not taste death before they see the kingdom of God come with power. (Mark 9:1)

This event was fulfilled when Jesus ascended to the throne. The outpouring of the Spirit signified the day the kingdom was officially opened to the public. The Day of Pentecost marked the establishment of the name of Jesus as the name above every other name and that day was celebrated with drunken glory!

The message of the 'Kingdom of God' came flooding back into the church in recent years after lying dormant for centuries. Once again, believers began to realize that the kingdom of God is the main message of Jesus. A new awareness has come and is breathing new life to believers all over the globe.

The Kingdom Teaching is sweeping through the body of Christ and is revolutionizing our efforts to take back the planet. There is a radical paradigm shift taking place because Jesus has been inaugurated. Instead of merely trying to get people to heaven, we are now positioning ourselves to bring heaven here!

Many believers have little understanding of what it means to actually live with this awareness. It seems to be a distant ideal instead of a present reality. The kingdom of God is a coming

---

[2] Ehrlich, Eugene. *Oxford American Dictionary.* New York: Oxford UP, 1980.

kingdom in the sense that it has not yet fully arrived. The kingdom is already but not yet.

What Does "Gospel" Mean?

Even the word 'gospel' needs to be redefined to its original meaning. Most Christians teach that the good news is that Jesus has died for us. That is definitely good news, but the original definition of the word "gospel" carries a much fuller meaning.

The angel said to them, "Do not be afraid. I bring you good news of great joy that will be for all the people. Today in the town of David a Savior has been born to you; he is Christ the Lord. (Luke 2:10-11)

The announcement of the angels was that a Savior has been born. The good news emphasized the birth of the Lord rather than His death. This same thought is echoed in the book of Isaiah: **"For to us a child is born, to us a son is given, and the government will be on his shoulders."** (Isaiah 9:6)

The Greek word for gospel, 'euangelion' was the good news of a royal birth or a stunning military victory.[3] The "gospel" speaks of events that establish a kingdom: a male heir is born to the throne and a military victory over an enemy. Jesus is born on earth and declared the new King and then conquers death and hell through his death, burial and resurrection. This good news

---

[3] Roop, John. "Sermon: 2 Advent 2008." Euangelion. Web. 09 May 2011. <http://rooppage.blogspot.com/2008/12/sermon-2-advent-2008.html>.

declares that Jesus is the royal Son of God born for us who has taken the government of God upon His shoulders.

Imagine in ancient times, a kingdom under the rule of a righteous, powerful ruler. Picture the joy of the people in this kingdom resting in a stable empire. But as the years go by, the king fails to produce a male offspring. And if you know anything about kingdoms, once the king dies, the kingdom goes into turmoil without a male heir.

As most of us were raised in democratic societies, the concept of a king and a kingdom are foreign to us. Yet in ancient times, they lived with a kingdom reality. Kingdoms were easily shaken at the death of their king. But if the king had a male heir to the throne, there was future security for the kingdom. The citizens were confident of a continual reign of righteousness, peace and joy, because a son would soon ascend to the throne and rule in the same spirit as his father.

In one of my favorite movies, "The Lion King," the animal kingdom is prospering, ruled under the Lion King, Mufasa. His son Simba is to be the next king and will rule in place of his father. However, Simba is young and foolish. His conniving uncle soon takes advantage of the situation.

Simba's Uncle Scar sets him up to believe that he killed his own father through his own carelessness. Simba was so shamed by this accusation that he leaves his territory, forfeiting the kingdom to his uncle. Shame drives him out of his calling and he ends up eating worms with a bunch of scavengers. The kingdom then crumbles under the uncle's weak leadership.

This is exactly what happens when God's people live as 'shamed sinners' instead of 'redeemed saints'. Guilt is a necessary tool to drive us to the cross, but shame must be scorned. Guilt says, "I made a mistake," but shame says, "I am a mistake." What did Jesus do? He, "...endured the cross, scorning its shame..." (Hebrews 12:2). Shame is the opposite of glory. We must not use the tool of shame to attempt build the kingdom of God.

Simba was radically transformed when he heard the voice of his Father from above saying, "Remember who you are. You are my son..." Once Simba heard His father's voice, he was empowered to take back the Kingdom of His father and rule righteously. That is what the father's blessing will do for us. It is the breath of life in our hearts that gives us the strength to succeed. I am reminded of God the Father as He blesses His Son Jesus saying, "This is my Son, whom I love; with him I am well pleased." (Matthew 3:17)

Blessing Fulfills Dynasty

The Hebrew word *barak* means, "to bless, to empower, to enable to succeed, to prosper, to be fertile, to live long." [4] "Blessing" words are not empty attempts at flattery, but are actually life giving words of power that are igniting destiny in the hearts of our children. Words are carriers. They carry faith or fear. As Proverbs 18:21, **"The tongue has the power of life and death, and those who love it will eat its fruit."**

---

[4] Zodhiates, Spiros, and John R. Kohlenberger. *The Hebrew-Greek Key Study Bible: New International Version.* Chattanooga, TN: AMG Pub., 1996. 1508.

Do you want to rule the kingdom? You must know who you are by hearing the Father's words over you. The greatest need in our societies is for the voice of the Father to be heard. I believe that very likely, the problems in our society are rooted in what I call, "the curse of fatherlessness." The very last verse in the Old Testament tells of the day when, **"He will turn the hearts of the fathers to their children, and the hearts of the children to their fathers; or else I will come and strike the land with a curse."** (Malachi 4:6)

God has chosen to reveal Himself as Father to show us His heart. He desires to pass on His mantle of authority to His Son. By embracing God as Father, we realize God is not wanting to hold *on* to His power- He wants to *give* it away to His sons. He is the ultimate risk taker.

Jesus is revealed as Son because He wants to show us how a faithful son responds when given authority and power. He points us to the Father, so that we will adore Him as He is adored by the Son. Jesus came to show us the protocol before the Father.

Every culture understands the impact of either a blessing or curse imparted through a father. I believe we must preach the good news in light of the Father Son relationship modeled for us in the New Testament. With Jesus as our example, we can follow in His steps and begin living as children of God.

Jesus' ministry began with His baptism, God's Spirit coming upon Him and a voice from heaven. This event as described in the book of Matthew:

The moment Jesus came up out of the baptismal waters, the skies opened up and he saw God's Spirit—it looked like a dove—descending and landing on him. And along with the Spirit, a voice: "This is my Son, chosen and marked by my love, delight of my life."
(Matthew 3:16-17 The Message)

For years I taught that baptism was the event that empowered the ministry of Jesus. The ritual or ceremony of being immersed in water to me was the main focus of that day. Today I have come to believe that it was not His baptism that enabled him to be released into ministry; rather it was His Father's blessing.

The pattern set for the life of Jesus, is the pattern we should set for our children. The father-son connection has been lost in many cultures, but as we look to the Jews, we find they have created a ceremony that has been passed on from generation to generation to preserve this connection. This ceremony is called a 'Bar Mitzvah'.

The 'Bar Mitzvah' is a part of Jewish culture that I wish all Christians could participate. The word 'Bar Mitzvah' means 'son of the law' and is a ceremony that brings boys into manhood. The 'Bar Mitvah' signifies the day the child becomes an adult and teaches the boy to embrace the laws of Moses. A powerful message of honor and generational blessing is imparted through this ceremony. Most of us have never understood the meaning behind the 'Bar Mitzvah', so we have labeled it a 'Jewish thing', instead of a 'God thing'.

I have seen many men run successful businesses, yet were unable to look their children directly in the eye to bless them. One of the most difficult things for a man to do is to bless his

19

children. The inner struggle within man to extend the blessing is rooted in his inability to give that which he has not received. This is unfortunate because the spoken blessing will transform a son or daughter into a prince or princess. A key to their heart resides in the spoken blessing of the father. This blessing releases the next generation the power to succeed.

Jabez cried out to the God of Israel, "Oh, that you would bless me and enlarge my territory! Let your hand be with me, and keep me from harm so that I will be free from pain." And God granted his request. (1 Chronicles 4:10)

Jabez passionately cried out for His Fathers blessing because he understood this would be the answer to his pain. The emotional pain that a fatherless generation suffers, creates a need for addictions that numb pain. Only the blessing of the father can heal this wound.

I have participated in spiritual warfare and have watched many Christians struggle to break off satanic curses over their lives. Once this was done, I often noticed their struggle still continued. I soon began to realize the root of our problem was not the curse as much as it was the lack of blessing. Remember, Jesus went straight to the wilderness and was victorious over the devil because He had the blessing of His Father. The power to effectively break curses and fight the devil rests in knowing who we are.

Sometimes I wonder if Hollywood is more open to God's message than His own people. I have discovered that many of the best-selling movies appeal to the hearts of people by showing them the power of a son fulfilling the work of his dad. Why would we not want to make this our emphasis as well? The pattern of heaven must become the pattern of earth.

I heard a story once about a group that decided to donate Mother's Day cards a couple of weeks before Mother's Day in a Federal Prison. The group could not keep the cards on the tables. The men of the prison were so grateful for the opportunity to send cards to their mothers.

Viewing the success of the day, they decided to do the same for Father's Day. To their surprise, no cards were taken that day. The men of the prison had no connection with their fathers, and therefore had no need to send a card. Was it the lack of a father that drove them into a life of crime? There is much evidence to prove this assumption.

The father's blessing is the key to success and is to be passed down to the next generation from the father. It was a common practice throughout the Bible for fathers to bless their sons, and for sons to seek the blessing of their father. Jacob blessed his sons.

Then he blessed Joseph and said, "May the God before whom my fathers Abraham and Isaac walked, the God who has been my shepherd all my life to this day, the Angel who has delivered me from all harm —may he bless these boys. May they be called by my name and the names of my fathers, Abraham and Isaac, and may they increase greatly upon the earth." (Genesis 48:15)

Our biblical forefathers understood the power of the father's blessing to bring about lasting success in the lives of their children. We have God as our model to teach us how to impart the blessing as fathers, and Jesus as our model to teach us how to receive it as sons and daughters. Many Christians have hardened their hearts to the need of the Father's love, because

21

they never received it from their earthly father. I am glad that God has the master key to our hearts, and we no longer have to rely on the blessing of our earthly father's alone. I believe God chose to reveal Himself as Our Father in heaven because He knew what our greatest need would be on earth.

Our enemy, the devil, realizes that without a strong father and son connection, everything will be lost. Future generations depend upon this relationship flourishing in families on earth once again! As it is in heaven, let it be on earth!

To me, the focus of the prodigal son story is much more about a loving father, rather than the rebellious son who spends his inheritance on prostitutes and alcohol. This is a well-told story, familiar to all. But a father, who runs to his son, kisses his neck, hugs him and throws a party for him: this son who had been living in shame; **that** is hard to believe! I think this parable should be more appropriately titled, 'The Loving Father'☐ instead of 'The Prodigal Son'. Our emphasis should be on the Father's amazing love for us, instead of the focus on our own shame. Read the words of Jesus again as I highlight the actions of the Father figure in this parable.

There was a man who had two sons. The younger one said to his father, "Father, give me my share of the estate." So he divided his property between them. Not long after that, the younger son got together all he had, set off for a distant country and there squandered his wealth in wild living. After he had spent everything, there was a severe famine in that whole country, and he began to be in need. So he went and hired himself out to a citizen of that country, who sent him to his fields to feed pigs. He longed to fill his stomach with the pods that the pigs were eating, but no one gave him anything. When he

came to his senses, he said, "How many of my father's hired men have food to spare, and here I am starving to death! I will set out and go back to my father and say to him: Father, I have sinned against heaven and against you. I am no longer worthy to be called your son; make me like one of your hired men." So he got up and went to his father. *But while he was still a long way off, his father saw him and was filled with compassion for him; he ran to his son, threw his arms around him and kissed him.* The son said to him, "Father, I have sinned against heaven and against you. I am no longer worthy to be called your son." But the father said to his servants, *"Quick! Bring the best robe and put it on him. Put a ring on his finger and sandals on his feet. Bring the fattened calf and kill it. Let's have a feast and celebrate. For this son of mine was dead and is alive again; he was lost and is found."* So they began to celebrate. (Luke 15:11-24)

The message found in this parable is difficult to receive by most people because of the shame they feel as sinners. Many people have a hard time understanding a father who runs to his son with arms wide open, even though the son squandered the family savings on prostitutes and gambling. The power of shame causes many to feel unworthy to be called a child of God. The power of forgiveness says, "This child was dead and is alive again! Let's party!"

Loved and Unashamed

I recently traveled to Asia and while there, I had the opportunity to teach on the Father's blessing. Like many other cultures, Asians are very driven by shame and false humility that is rooted deep in their family traditions. For example, it is common in Chinese culture for a father to disagree with someone who might compliment how pretty his little girl is. He will disagree in fear of his daughter becoming prideful. I think this is actually a kind of false humility.

Many Asian cultures will push their children to succeed and shame them if they do not perform well. Shaming a child, or labeling them, creates great confusion, because it connects performance with identity. Shame releases the fear of failure. Never curse identity in an attempt to correct behavior. A child's true identity should never be put into question or tied to performance.

Shame keeps us from being powerful! Paul said, **"I am not ashamed of the gospel, because it is the power of God."** (Romans 1:16) Where there is shame, there is powerlessness. That is why Jesus "scorned the shame."

Let us fix our eyes on Jesus, the author and perfecter of our faith, who for the joy set before him endured the cross, scorning its shame, and sat down at the right hand of the throne of God. (Hebrews 12:2)

Jesus endured the hardship, but did not let it shame him, even though death on the cross is the most humiliating death imaginable. The crucifixion tortured its victims and degraded them, hanging them naked on a tree, nailed like a billboard on a public roadway for display. Our shame became His, and He brought us to glory through what He suffered.

In bringing many sons to glory, it was fitting that God, for whom and through whom everything exists, should make the author of their salvation perfect through suffering. (Hebrews 2:10)

24

Shame is the opposite of glory. When we walk in shame, we have allowed lies to mark our identity. Conversely, when we walk in glory, we are walking with our adoption papers in hand, declaring that we are sons and daughters, loved and delighted in by the Father. When we begin to see the power of shame and its destructive nature to the kingdom, we must then resist our earthly nature to use shame. I find that very often, if you are using shame in your relationships, you are also living in shame. Whether we find it in ourselves, or in others, shame distorts and dehumanizes the soul. Shame dominates any mind it invades, and like an infection, weakens our immune system to sin.

God reveals Himself as Father first and foremost. Even in the Old Testament, we find prophecies pointing to God raising up His Son to continue His dynasty:

Return to us, God Almighty! Look down from heaven and see! Watch over this vine, the root your right hand has planted, *the son you have raised up for yourself.* **Your vine is cut down, it is burned with fire; at your rebuke your people perish.** *Let your hand rest on the man at your right hand, the son of man you have raised up for yourself.* **Then we will not turn away from you; revive us, and we will call on your name. Restore us, LORD God Almighty; make your face shine on us, that we may be saved.** (Psalm 80:14-19 italics mine)

The gospel is the message of God sending His Son to complete His work on earth. Jesus is not God per se, but God's Son, who is in every way like His Father. Jesus obeyed the Father by going to the cross and removing our sin and shame, trading our shame for His glory. Sonship is the privilege we receive when we believe in God's Son, Jesus. **"Yet to all who did receive him, to those who believed in his name, he gave the right to become children of God..."** (John 1:12)

Remember the great glory you felt when you first received Jesus as Lord? That glory is found only when you recognize your rights as a son or daughter. An example of this glory is found in the Bar Mitzvah. Every Jewish boy participates in this public ceremony that declares and seals his sonship. Jewish culture also declares that the names of the father were included as part of the name of the son.

Jesus replied, "Blessed are you, Simon son of Jonah, for this was not revealed to you by flesh and blood, but by my Father in heaven." (Matthew 16:17)

The son and father were so connected in ancient times that Simon (or Peter) was known as "Simon son of Jonah." How much more must we acknowledge the Father's connection to His Son Jesus as the foundation of our message as Christians!

In the next chapter, we will begin to take a deeper look at the scientific language we use in our theology. By using terms void of relational language, we miss out on the obvious message of a Father blessing His Son, and a Son entering into manhood. To accomplish our goal, we must take a look at the formation of the church in the early centuries of Christianity.

Reflection

1. Heaven's Dynasty describes a kingdom that continues on to the next generation. How does this concept apply to Jesus?

2. The Greek word for gospel, *euangelion* was defined as 'the good news of a royal birth or a stunning military victory.' How does this definition differ from your understanding of the message of the gospel?

3. Name some ways that you see the 'curse of fatherlessness' effecting our families, the body of Christ and entire cultures.

4.   Take a moment and say your name as 'son of _____' (insert the name of your father). If you are a parent, use this same concept in referring to your children. What message does this communicate?

5. Watch "The Lion King" and discuss the power of dynasty as it relates to Jesus and the Father.

chapter two
Uncomplicated
Love

I wrote a song a number of years ago that is called 'Simply I Come'. I wrote the song because, as a worship leader, I recognized how easily I could complicate the simple pleasure of enjoying God! The chorus of the song says:

Simply I come, with a child-like faith, with a child-like love,
with a child-like praise. Simply I come, with uncompromised faith,
with uncomplicated love, with a simple song of praise, I come.

I love to think deeply, but at the same time I try to convey things as simply as possible. Every week I stand before a couple of hundred people and present the gospel as clearly and as powerfully as I am able. I gave up years ago trying to impress people with knowledge. I seek to make my message as user friendly as possible, which requires me to examine carefully the words I use.

Christians often speak what I call 'Christianese'. We use terms that most of the world does not understand. When I preach the gospel, I preach in blue jeans, with a cup of coffee and with language that the world easily understands.

My heart's desire is to communicate the truth of God's Word to a dying world. This journey requires me to examine the road taken by the church through the last two millenniums. I think we must make some structural changes in our foundations to accommodate the kingdom of God here on earth.

The Need for Creed?

There was a shift in emphasis that occurred when the church and the Roman Empire joined forces. As Christianity became culturally accepted, Christians conformed to Roman culture in their thought patterns. It is my observation that the emphasis shifted from lifestyle to doctrine, from how we live, to how we think, and from the language of covenant and relationship, to the language of philosophy, math and science.

These formal statements of faith were designed to protect Christianity from error. Truth exists within the creeds, yes, but there is also an emphasis in the Creeds that shift us from a Biblical emphasis. One of the earliest Creeds from the fourth century A.D. states,

We believe in one God, the Father Almighty, Maker of all things visible and invisible. And in one Lord Jesus Christ, the Son of God, begotten of the Father [the only-begotten; that is, of the essence of the Father, God of

God], Light of Light, very God of very God, begotten, not made, being of one substance with the Father;
First Council of Nicea (325)[1]

While I believe this language is unnecessarily complicated, I also recognize that the intent was to bring unity among the believers. I certainly appreciate the devotion to bring unity through the creeds because, when we focus on our differences, our differences become the focus instead of that which unites us; Jesus Christ as Lord. One scholar stated, *"The Nicene-Constantinopolitan Creed seems dramatically different from the Christians' first simple exclamation, "Jesus is Lord."*[2]

The Roman emperor summoned the Council of Nicea in 325 A.D. as a reaction to the controversy in doctrine among the early Christians. At the Council of Nicea, distinct observations formed in the mind of Christians that have kept the faith orthodox, but not necessarily with the correct Biblical emphasis.

The Result of Resisting Jewish Roots

I began to question the language of the Creeds because of the emphasis placed upon rules and doctrine, instead of faith and passion. Remember that all of the authors of Scripture were Jewish, except for Luke, who wrote the gospel of Luke, the book of Acts, and possibly the letter to the Hebrews. Yet out of

---

[1] "Nicene Creed." *Wikipedia, the Free Encyclopedia.* Web. 16 Feb. 2011. <http://en.wikipedia.org/wiki/Nicene_Creed>.
[2] Johnson, Luke Timothy. *The Creed: What Christians Believe and Why It Matters.* New York: Doubleday, 2003. 38.

the three hundred and eighteen bishops that were invited to the councils to form the Creeds of the church, not one was of Jewish descent. From the very formation of what most of the church says is orthodoxy, (i.e. correct theology) we find an element missing that is vital for a Biblical foundation: Jewish influence.

By the time of the Councils, most of the leadership in the church had rejected any Jewish influence. I believe that the seeds of Anti-Semitism were first planted in the hearts of the Christians of Rome. The church lacked an understanding of honoring the Jewish people and neglected the goal of Jew and Gentile becoming one in Christ. I believe this rejection resulted in a spiritual blindness over many of the early Christian leaders that continues even today.

This spiritual blindness became very clear to me one day. I remember looking over a class syllabus on the book of Romans presented by a former seminary teacher. He basically skipped over chapters nine, ten, and eleven, as if Romans only had thirteen chapters! These three chapters are essential in understanding our connection with Israel. Yet this professor could not grasp their relevancy because of his own spiritual blindness.

I believe that the church must have a heart for Israel! Paul said, **"For I could wish that I myself were cursed and cut off from Christ for the sake of my people, those of my own race."** (Romans 9:3). Paul interceded for Israel because he understood their importance as a nation in God's eyes. For three chapters of this letter, Paul very specifically discusses the proper view of Gentile and Jew. By the spirit of God, he addresses the Gentiles concerning their arrogance as a "mere branch" because they had not respected the Jewish people as "the root."

If some of the branches have been broken off, and you, though a wild olive shoot, have been grafted in among the others and now share in the nourishing sap from the olive root, do not boast over those branches. If you do, consider this: You do not support the root, but the root supports you. (Romans 11:17-18)

Consider the rejection of Jewish influence in the early church and its consequences. A branch separated from "nourishing sap' will not survive! The true body of Christ will be a result of Jew and Gentile coming together as "one new man."

Remember that at that time you (non-Jews) were separate from Christ, excluded from citizenship in Israel and foreigners to the covenants of the promise, without hope and without God in the world. But now in Christ Jesus you who once were far away have been brought near through the blood of Christ. For he himself is our peace, who has made the two one and has destroyed the barrier, the dividing wall of hostility, by abolishing in his flesh the law with its commandments and regulations. His purpose was to create in himself one new man out of the two, thus making peace, and in this one body to reconcile both of them to God through the cross, by which he put to death their hostility. (Ephesians 2:12-16 italics mine)

Unfortunately, Paul's warnings went unheeded and the church was left without a Jewish perspective of the kingdom of God. I believe the result led to a complication of the language in which we use to define God and the perspective in which we view Him.

33

The church began a course in which they united with the Roman Empire, instead of with the Jewish brethren. The body of Christ had been persecuted for over two hundred years by different emperors of Rome, but in the early fourth century, the persecution was halted through the Edict of Milan. A little more than a decade later, a Roman emperor took the prominent role in influencing the direction of the Christian world. His name was Constantine.

Constantine Inconsistency

Constantine was impacted by Christ through a vision he had before going into battle to conquer Rome. Through this vision he was prompted to paint the sign of the cross on the shields of his soldiers. Constantine won a decisive victory during the battle for Rome, giving him complete rule over the western half of the Roman Empire. Constantine became the first Christian emperor of Rome.

Next to the resurrection of Christ, many scholars consider Constantine's conversion the most significant event in human history.[3] He was an influential and successful emperor in many aspects, and presided over the Council of Nicea, the first of seven councils that helped formulate Christian doctrine.

Constantine involved himself in religious matters and heavily controlled the outcomes of these councils. Can you imagine the president or leader of your country making doctrinal decisions

---

[3] Carroll, James. *Constantine's Sword: the Church and the Jews : a History*. Boston: Houghton Mifflin, 2001. 171

that would govern the body of Christ? Would you want these decisions then to be enforced by the government? Not me!

We should also consider the lifestyle of Constantine. Historians claim that this man poisoned his eldest son Crispus, and also killed one of his wives within two years after the first Council of Nicea.[4] It is possible that God used this man in spite of his character, however, Constantine's influence over the body of Christ seemed to defile it instead of revive it.

Constantine most likely involved himself in church doctrine in order to keep the empire united. The body of Christ at that time was deeply divided over how one defines the person of Jesus Christ.

I recently watched the movie "The Clash of the Titans." In this movie there are gods who sit in the heavenlies and descend upon mankind, sometimes even to conceive a child. In the time of the early church, most of the population perceived God (or the gods) from this perspective. This view was often carried into their understanding of who Jesus was. Was He God? Was He a demi-God? How could God be one and Jesus be God? Yet many of these questions were being asked from a wrong perspective and cannot be answered correctly from a Greek philosophical mindset. A Jewish perspective is necessary, but was not included in the formation of the Creeds, because Jews were not included in the discussion.

Therefore, since the fourth century, we have inherited

---

[4] Ibid,. 203.

doctrine that has bred confusion, because the Church has not sought the Hebraic understanding of scriptures. A Greek philosophical background replaced the Jewish understanding of the Early Church. Instead of scripture releasing people into the kingdom of light, the church entered into a millennium of darkness following the establishment of the Creeds.

In our discussion of the Creeds, I must make a disclaimer: *Creeds may have been a necessary means of securing a proper, exalted view of Christ.* At that time in history, very few people had access to the Scriptures and most even lacked the education to read. These ancient proclamations may have been the means of providing a ground wire to the Word of God for many Christians.

In making this disclaimer, I hope that we can gain proper perspective of our past and move on to reveal the heart of the gospel message. I am more concerned with the language of these proclamations than I am with the content. The Creeds must bow to the revelation of Scripture and should conform to its language, not vice versa.

God is *not* a Substance

In Greek philosophy, the very first question that had to be answered was, "What is the substance or essence of all things?" Philosophical ideas soon penetrated Christian theology and the simplicity of a Father Son relationship became complicated. God became a substance.

The Trinity can only be understood once this idea is firmly established. The Father is made of God substance as well as the Son and the Spirit. Each is fully its own person but is also

100% pure God substance and completely God. The Trinity represented what theologians call 'the Godhead': three persons of one divine substance.

The introduction of philosophy and Greek thought added unbiblical vocabulary to the church. Neither Jesus nor any of the New Testament writers ever addressed God as a substance. Conflict and confusion continued amongst church leaders in the early church.

In the year 359 AD, Church leaders once again debated the conclusions that were arrived at by the Council of Nicea. I discovered this quote in a book entitled, *Documents of The Early Church*:

But the term 'essence' has been taken up by the Fathers rather unwisely, and gives offense because it is not understood by the people. It is also not contained in the Scriptures. For these reasons we have decided to do away with it, and that no use at all shall be made of it or in the future in connection with God, because the divine Scriptures nowhere use it of the Father and the Son. But we say that the Son is like the Father in all things, as the Holy Scriptures say and teach.[5] (Soc. H.E. ii 37; Ath. De syn.8)

The early church debated questions not even addressed in the Bible, which then established the foundations of philosophy. Throughout the next few chapters you will see why I believe we must un-complicate our minds and simply receive the words of the Bible. The simple relational language of Father and Son

---

[5] Bettenson, Henry Scowcroft. *Documents of the Christian Church*. New York: Oxford UP, 1947. 61.

provide us with the true revelation of who Jesus really is: the very Son of God!

I believe the root of the problem lies in this: the relationship of Jesus to the Father should be viewed through the eye of a first century Jew.... not a first century Greek philosopher! We complicate the relationship between the Father and the Son by using terminology not found in the scriptures.

If we are asking questions about the substance of the Father, of Jesus, and of the Holy Spirit, perhaps we are asking the wrong questions. This then leads us to conclusions that were not emphasized in the Early Church. In my view, the question should simply ask, "What is Jesus' relationship to the Father?" with the simple truth in reply, "He is His Son."

Emphasize Jesus as Lord

In light of this understanding of the word "God" and the revelation it carries with it, let us examine some other texts. God is not seen as a substance in Scripture, but rather refers to a title that is given. This is why Jesus responded to the Pharisees in this manner:

Is it not written in your law, I said, "You are gods?" If He called them gods, to whom the word of God came (and the Scripture cannot be broken), do you say of Him whom the Father sanctified and sent into the world, "You are blaspheming," because I said, "I am the Son of God?" (John 10:34-36)

Scripture declares there are many gods, but that there is no other God except ONE. Why else would Yahweh be called the

Most High God if there were no other gods to rule over? The position of a god refers to a position of ruling; nothing more and nothing less. Yet today, when someone is identified in this culture as 'god', we think of him or her as being elevated to the 'substance' of divinity. But with the substance argument out of the way, this language becomes less offensive and more accurate. Many times I find that words are the least effective form of communication- especially religious words!

Even Christ did not assign to Himself the job description of God. Luke 18:19 says, **"'Why do you call me good?' Jesus answered. 'No one is good-except God alone.'"**

He most often identified Himself as the Son of God, Son of Man or the Messiah. The disciples point to Jesus as Lord or *Adonai* in Hebrew. The Jews and Christians share the same exact God; whom we call Yahweh. Because of the blood of Jesus, *all* who receive Jesus Christ have the right to become sons of God.

One day I asked the Lord why the name Yahweh is not used in the New Testament. I heard Him say, "What do your children call you? Do they call you by your first name, or Dad?" I then realized why we do not use the name 'Yahweh' much. Instead we call Him 'Father,' just as you would expect your children to call you. Actually, I believe Yahweh wants His children to call him 'Abba, Father,' like Jesus said in his most desperate hour, **"Abba Father, everything is possible for you."** (Mark 14:36)

What was the message in the book of Acts? Was it to declare, "Jesus is God" or "Jesus is Lord?" If we claim that Jesus is God, we infer that Jesus is the Father. I believe this idea opens the door to much confusion. The following is a list of scriptures found in the book of Acts that show the message of the first Christians was "Jesus is Lord" not "Jesus is God".

Therefore let all Israel be assured of this: God has made this Jesus, whom you crucified, both Lord and Christ. (Acts 2:36)

With great power the apostles continued to testify to the resurrection of the Lord Jesus, and much grace was upon them all. (Acts 4:33)

While they were stoning him, Stephen prayed, "Lord Jesus, receive my spirit." (Acts 7:59)

You know the message God sent to the people of Israel, telling the good news of peace through Jesus Christ, who is Lord of all. (Acts 10:36)

So if God gave them the same gift as he gave us, who believed in the Lord Jesus Christ, who was I to think that I could oppose God? (Acts 11:17)

Some of them, however, men from Cyprus and Cyrene, went to Antioch and began to speak to Greeks also, telling them the good news about the Lord Jesus. (Acts 11:20)

No! We believe it is through the grace of our Lord Jesus that we are saved, just as they are. (Acts 15:11)

..men who have risked their lives for the name of our Lord Jesus Christ. (Acts 15:26)

They replied, "Believe in the Lord Jesus, and you will be saved—you and your household." (Acts 16:31)

He had been instructed in the way of the Lord, and he spoke with great fervor and taught about Jesus accurately, though he knew only the baptism of John. (Acts 18:25)

On hearing this, they were baptized into the name of the Lord Jesus. (Acts 19:5)

Some Jews who went around driving out evil spirits tried to invoke the name of the Lord Jesus over those who were demon-possessed. They would say, "In the name of Jesus, whom Paul preaches, I command you to come out." (Acts 19:13)

When this became known to the Jews and Greeks living in Ephesus, they were all seized with fear, and the name of the Lord Jesus was held in high honor. (Acts 19:17)

I cannot ask people to merely *believe* in God. People of many diverse faiths *believe* in God. But James, 2:19 says, **"You believe that there is one God. Good! Even the demons believe that—and shudder."** The confession that brings salvation is the acknowledgement of God's Son Jesus Christ. Romans 10:9 says, **"If you confess with your mouth Jesus is Lord, and believe in your heart that God raised him from the dead, you will be saved."**

I believe that our emphasis in evangelism and teaching must be that Jesus is Lord, *not* that Jesus is God. The Book of Daniel 7:13-14 reminds us that Jesus has been given authority, glory and sovereign power, and that all peoples and nations would worship Him. Jesus is not the Ancient of Days, yet He is revered in the same manner.

In my vision at night I looked, and there before me was one like a son of man, coming with the clouds of heaven. He approached the Ancient of Days and was led into his presence. He was given authority, glory and sovereign power; all peoples, nations and men of every language worshiped him. His dominion is an everlasting dominion that will not pass away, and his kingdom is one that will never be destroyed. (Daniel 7:13-14)

These verses in the book of Daniel clearly show **"one like a son of man"** approaching **"the Ancient of Days"** to be given authority, glory and sovereign power and to be worshiped. Jesus referred to Himself repeatedly as "the Son of Man" throughout His ministry. Listen to His words in Mark 10:45, **"For even the Son of Man did not come to be served, but to serve, and to give his life as a ransom for many."** Jesus is the son of man in the book of Daniel who was led into the presence of the Ancient of Days. What a testimony to the Jew!

As Christians, we must be as Biblically accurate with our understanding of God as possible. Let us take the mystery out of 'who Jesus is' and 'who God is.' We need to present the truth in simplicity and with clarity: Jesus is the Son of God who is ruling the throne of Yahweh his Father.

Jesus was much more of a Messiah than the Jews ever expected. They believed He would be a leader like Moses. Instead, He came declaring Himself to be "the Son of God." Jesus is one with the Father; therefore, as we worship the Father, we also worship the Son. Jesus is doing the work of the Father here on earth and will reign until everything is subjected

42

to His Father. Once His work is complete, He too, will subject Himself to the Father, so that God may be all in all.

Much is at stake in this matter, especially when we think of evangelism. Confusion will only drive away Jews, Muslims and other God seekers from the truth. The words, "Godhead, divinity and trinity," hinder the real message of the kingdom. Now is the time for boldness and clarity in our message! Remember the acronym K.I.S.S. Keep it simple saint! In the next chapter we will discuss the power of the paradigm shift that often precedes understanding.

Reflection

1. Why do you think we have a tendency to complicate that which God has made for our simple pleasure?
2. Early Greek thinkers began with the question, "What is the substance or essence of all things?" Should Christianity follow in the footsteps of philosophy and begin with the same question?
3. Why don't we use the name of Yahweh very much in our worship as Christians?
4. Does Scripture emphasize that "Jesus is God" or "Jesus is Lord"?

chapter three
Shifting Paradigms

One day a lady went into an automotive store and told them she needed a 710 cap. She adamantly claimed that every engine had such a cap and demanded the clerk retrieve her one immediately. Clueless, the clerk took her to the car, opened the hood and asked the woman to show him exactly where this cap was located. Sure enough, she pointed right on top of the engine to the cap. To his surprise, there it was...the "710" cap! Or, turned upside down, the "OIL" cap! This story is a good example of a shift in paradigm.

Since the very beginning of Christianity, there have been two different patterns of thinking; Hellenistic and Hebraic. These two patterns of thought do not conform to one another and will always be in conflict. A thought process or pattern is a way of thinking, or worldview, that will redefine every fact or piece of information that enters into its system.

The definition of paradigm is "a typical example or pattern of something; a model."[1] A paradigm is the backdrop on the stage of your life; the scenery behind the actors in the movie. Often the paradigm is so much in the background that it goes unnoticed. A paradigm is like a pair of colored sunglasses that color everything in your view.

The best way I can explain a paradigm is as follows: Imagine trying to play football on a baseball field. You are trying to follow the rules of football, but nothing seems to fit together. Move the teams to a football field, and everything just seems to fit.

Paradigm shifts take place in the business realm, political realm, and in the kingdom. Many times the shift takes place because of new ideas and revelations that are discovered. In the 18th century, a movement called 'Nationalism' began to spread. This movement emphasized loyalty to one's nation instead of to a particular city or political leader. Nationalism sparked both the American and French Revolutions. It brought people together, breeding oneness and loyalty under one power.

Paradigm shifts may be sparked by new inventions or technologies. The Internet has connected the world together and has forced us to think beyond our own geographical area.

---

[1] Ehrlich, Eugene. *Oxford American Dictionary*. New York: Oxford UP, 1980.

This innovation is actually bringing the world back together in a way that no one could have imagined.

Most scientists believe the landmass of the earth was once one huge continent. This land mass was called *Pangaea*. Imagine everyone having access to one another without having to cross a large mass of water! But the continents soon began to drift apart in a phenomenon called the 'continental drift'. This 'drift' is alluded to in scripture:

Two sons were born to Eber: One was named Peleg, because in his time the earth was divided. (Genesis 10:25)

Consider how the Internet has reconnected what was divided, creating a new *Pangaea* to our world. The new technology releases a paradigm shift because it is rooted in creativity, and creativity is rooted in God. The first action of our God was creativity. **"In the beginning God created..."** (Genesis 1:1).

Kingdom Paradigm Shift

In the same way that new technologies spark a paradigm shift, new revelations will do the same. I firmly believe that a second Reformation is at hand. Every five hundred years there seems to be a theological shift in the church back to her roots. On October 31, 1517, Martin Luther nailed his ninety-five theses on a door and sparked a reformation. The printing press was the invention that enabled his ideas to reach the common people. Today we have the resources of the Internet to facilitate the next reformation. Get ready!

A paradigm shift must always begin with first recognizing the roots of our beliefs systems and a willingness to re-examine why we believe what we believe. The word 'radical' has been defined as *"relating to the root of something."*[2] I want to be a radical in the sense of returning to the roots of our faith, because the root provides the nourishment needed for life! The idea of being radical, actually defines us as those who are living the way we were created, or rooted to live and believe.

The biggest hindrance to living out this radical mindset comes from having the wrong paradigm to begin with. We find ourselves stuck in a system of beliefs that actually hinders God's Word from working in our lives. This is why Jesus calls us to 'repent'.

The word 'repent' is the Greek word *metanoe,* which means to change your paradigm. *Meta* means 'change' and *noe* means 'mind' or 'way of thinking.'[3] Yet most people think of repentance, in the context of, first, having an emotional response to their sin, and secondly, turning away from their ungodly lifestyle. True repentance causes us to go to a higher place, viewing life from God's perspective instead of our own. Remember that Jesus said that repentance, or a paradigm shift is required before you can believe.

"The time has come," he said. "The kingdom of God is near. Repent and believe the good news!" (Mark 1:15)

In the time of Jesus, there was a movement that spread

---

[2] Ehrlich, Eugene. *Oxford American Dictionary.* New York: Oxford UP, 1980.

[3] Zodhiates, Spiros, and John R. Kohlenberger. *The Hebrew-Greek Key Study Bible: New International Version.* Chattanooga, TN: AMG Pub., 1996. 1508.

throughout the world called Hellenism. This mindset was literally forced upon all the conquered people during the reign of Alexander the Great and the kings who followed him. Hellenism is a paradigm shift or mindset that opposes the Biblical paradigm. I will refer to Hellenism as 'Greek thought' and the Biblical paradigm, 'Hebraic thought.'

If you were born in America, or part of Western civilization, you have a Hellenistic paradigm. Let me give you a few examples: the Biblical day begins as the sun *sets* in Jewish culture. The book of Genesis says, **"God called the light 'day,' and the darkness he called 'night.' And there was evening, and there was morning-the first day."** In Greek thought, the day began at midnight and ended at midnight. You wake up in the morning and exclaim, "Ah, a new day!" In Hebraic thought, the Jew exclaims once he is able to see three stars in the sky after sunset, "Ah, a new day!"

Greek thought assumes we eat at 8:00am, noon and 6:00pm. Hebraic thought assumes we eat when we are hungry. Greek thought pictures time as a time line, which never ends. Hebraic thought sees time as a circle and everything has a season. Greek thought sees the future as ahead of us. Hebraic thought sees the past in front of us and we are backing into the future, similar to a person rowing a rowboat.

When Scriptures refer to the hand of God, the Greek mind sees five fingers and a palm. In Hebrew thought, the function of the hand, not the form, is what is considered.

I want to point out these distinctions of thought because most of us have not even considered our paradigm or mindset. Jesus used the word *repent* as the key that would unlock the door to the kingdom of God. We can change our paradigm!

Differing Paradigms Produce Conflict

A major problem in the body of Christ is that many have cried over their sins, but have not assumed a new mindset. Though repentance does relate to godly sorrow, it also assumes a transformation of thought. Without this transformation, conflict will arise. What was the first conflict among believers?

And in these days, the disciples multiplying, there came a murmuring of the Hellenists at the Hebrews, because their widows were being overlooked in the daily ministration... (Acts 6:1 Young's Literal Translation)

The Hellenists were Jews who had a Greek thought process, and the Hebrews were Jews who had a Hebraic thought process. Most translations do not translate the word Hellenists, even though it is found in the Greek text.

As I reflected on this portion of scripture, I felt the Spirit of God point out to me that differing mindsets and paradigms fuel all conflict in the body of Christ. Think of fellowships that embrace the miraculous and those who do not. This conflict is based on differing paradigms. Greek thought elevates reason. However, miracles do not operate according to reason. Christians are divided at this point, even though they all confess Jesus as Lord. What many Christians lack is a paradigm shift that unlocks the fullness of the kingdom of God upon their lives.

As a teacher, I am persuaded that my most important job is to impact the paradigm of my listeners. I must not become merely a storyteller or fact giver. A paradigm shift must take place.

I believe we should leave behind the paradigm that says we must view God from a philosophical mindset. The word theology means, "the study of the nature of God." But I believe that our goal as Christians is not to study His nature, but rather to have relationship with Him.

I call this paradigm shift, "P.S. I Love You." P.S. stands for *Paradigm Shift*, and *"I Love You"* is the emphasis. John tells us, **"We love because he first loved us."** (1 John 4:19) Think about it. He loved us first! I often refrain from singing how much "I" love God because the truth is; "I" have trouble believing how much He loves me. Once I can receive *His* love for me, then I am empowered to love! I must emphasize His love for me over my love for Him.

Theology has the tendency to place what you believe in your mind over how you live from your heart. European philosophers of past centuries have emphasized the mind over the heart. Rene' Descartes, a well- known 17th Century philosopher, is known for saying "cogito ergo sum." [4](English: "I **think**, therefore I am") I take issue with this. Our being is not rooted in how *we* think, but in how we *receive* the love of the Father.

We are called to be loved by God. "I am loved by God, therefore I am!" Our being is satisfied in being a beloved son and daughter of the King. Studying God may bring understanding, but understanding will never satisfy our souls.

---

[4] Palmer, Donald. *Looking at Philosophy: the Unbearable Heaviness of Philosophy Made Lighter*. Mountain View, CA: Mayfield Pub., 1994. 162.

Our intellectual pursuit will blind us from our true purpose of being. We must repent therefore, and be loved by God!

Once we embrace this paradigm shift, we can then love Him. As Jesus said, in Luke 10:27:

"Love the Lord your God with all your heart and with all your soul and with all your strength and with all your mind;" and, " Love your neighbor as yourself."

Only when we let God love us, can we truly love our neighbor and love Him. Many accuse us of self-love, and I believe rightly so!

Not only should we love God with all our hearts, but also with all of our minds. *We must not become mindless charismatics, or heartless intellectuals!* There is a ditch on either side of the road. Study His word and meditate on His ways, but find your satisfaction in loving God and being loved by Him.

Knowledge puffs up, but love builds up. The man who thinks he knows something does not yet know as he ought to know. But the man who loves God is known by God. (1 Corinthians 8:1-3)

In the next few chapters, I will go into greater detail of how we ought to relate to God as Father, Jesus as Son, and His Spirit as our connection to them and to one another.

Reflection

1. How does the word 'repent' connect with the idea of a paradigm shift?

2. To experience a paradigm shift, go out at dusk, and the moment you see three stars in the sky, announce, "Ah! A new day!" Ponder how this shift would effect the way you celebrate the New Year or a birthday.

3. Describe the impact of Rene' Descartes statement, "I think, therefore I am," versus the thought, "I am loved by God, therefore I am!"

4. How do we avoid becoming either mindless charismatics or heartless intellectuals?

chapter four
God Defined

*I*slam is spreading throughout the world today. Their view of God rejects first and foremost the idea of God being a Father and having a Son. Yet, this idea of God as Father is the message of the Bible. Even in the Old Testament, Yahweh said to the nation of Israel, **"I thought you would call me 'Father' and not turn away from following me."** (Jeremiah 3:19)

Islam focuses on the greatness of God. They continually say, "Allah Akbar" which means "God is great!" This is a true statement, but misses the mark. Islam creates an image of God as a distant, cold and demanding King, who is inaccessible, yet desires extreme ceremonial devotion. Their God does not require a heart change toward other races, women or toward their enemies. The only requirement is devotion to "Allah" (which is the Arabic word for God) and to his prophet

55

Mohammed.

Islam is based on many lies about the nature and character of God, especially His nature as a loving Father. In direct opposition, Christianity declares that God *is* a Father and He *has* a Son that has ascended to the throne. Islam cries out, "Far be it from God that He should have a Son!"[1] These very words encircle the Dome of the Rock Mosque in Jerusalem.

Jesus as the *son,* as the heir to the throne, is the message so vehemently opposed by not only the Muslims, but by much of the world. But to be critical of Islam without checking our own hearts would be a mistake. Many Christians treat God as great, yet do not interact with Him as a Father.

If our approach toward God is not based on the view of "Abba, Father," we may fall back into distancing ourselves from His greatness. Jesus came to earth, to say, "Yes, God is great!," but more importantly, that "He wants relationship with you!" It is easy to believe that God is great, but difficult to believe He is in a good mood toward us.

In the next few chapters, I want to define the word "God" in the way I believe the word was meant to be defined. The concept of the kingdom of God as a dynasty continuing through the Son, hinges on some basic thoughts we have about who God is to us. Let me list a few of my basic assumptions:

---

[1] The Qur'an, which is the holy book of Islam says: "Verily Allah is only One. Glorified be he, than that he should ever have a son. To him is everything in the heavens and on the earth. And sufficient is Allah as an overseer." (Surah 4:171)

1. God is a Title or Job Description
2. God is *not* His name
3. God is *not* a substance or essence
4. Yahweh is God's name
5. Jesus is God's Son

Many theologians have lost the simplicity of the message by using complicated language. Let's begin by digging into the meaning of the personal name of God.

God has a Personal Name

Many Bible teachers teach that God has many names, but in fact He has only one name. The four letters that make up this name, YHWH, are called the Tetragrammaton. Jews for centuries have refrained from ever saying the holy name of God in fear of being irreverent. When reading the Torah, rabbis would say 'LORD' instead of the Tetragrammaton.

'Yahweh' is the most common way to pronounce the these four Hebrew letters, yet others have used the pronunciation 'Jehovah.' The true pronunciation of God's name has been forgotten. Since Hebrew was a spoken language more than a written language, vowels were not placed in the texts until about the sixth century A.D. With only the consonants placed in the Hebrew text, we are left with only a guess of how to pronounce His name.

What many Bible teachers refer to as the 'Names of God,' are better identified as His job descriptions. YHWH Rapha would not be another name for God, but instead it declares His job description as "Yahweh who heals." Yahweh Shalom describes Him as the "Yahweh who brings Peace." The same idea can be seen in the name Jesus Christ. 'Jesus' is the name of the Son of God and 'Christ' describes His job description as Messiah or Christ.

God is not His name! Modern Christianity has elevated the word 'God' in terms that make Christianity more confusing than convincing. Yahweh is God's name and Jesus is the name of His Son.

We say sometimes that, "There is no high like the Most High." Second Samuel 22:14 declares, **"The LORD thundered from heaven; the voice of the Most High resounded."** Yahweh is called the Most High God because He is higher than all other gods. God is a title given to one who rules. There would be no need for a Most High God if there were not lesser gods as well.

Creative Language Pictures

To help better understand the proper meaning of the word "God," we will take a closer look at the Hebrew language. Linguists have discovered the Hebrew alphabet was once a pictorial language. This means that every letter of the Hebrew alphabet was actually a picture or drawing of an object that it represented.

For instance, the first letter of the Hebrew alphabet was the

A – the *aleph*. This letter was a picture of an ox head, which meant "strength." The second letter of the Hebrew alphabet was the B – the *bet*. The B was the picture of a house or a tent. By combining the *aleph* and the *bet*, we see a word picture of a "strong house" or "the strength of the house," which is the Hebrew word for 'Father.' (Note as well that by combining the first two letters of the Hebrew alphabet we have aleph bet, or alphabet or alephbet)

The word for God in Hebrew is 'EL' spelled *aleph, lahmed*. The L is the *lahmedh*, which is a picture of a staff and represents "one who rules, or shepherds." The word picture for "EL" is a "strong ruler" or "shepherd."[2] When we say 'God,' El is the picture we should hold in our mind.

The word for son in Hebrew is 'BEN' spelled, *bet, nun*. The *bet* is the picture of a house or tent and the *nun* is a picture of a seed. The son is the seed to continue the house and carry on the dynasty into future. Jesus is the Son of God and Heaven's dynasty is completed through his rule!

---

[2] *Ancient Hebrew Research Center - Home Page*. Web. 16 Oct. 2010. <http://www.ancient-hebrew.org/>.

Relational Language Only

As we understand that God is not to be thought of as a substance, but as a job description, we begin to eliminate the confusion that is often experienced in trying to explain the relationship between the Father and the Son. God holds the position of ruling in which the Father and the Son operate.

Once we release the need to determine the substance of God and the substance of Jesus, we are free to understand the simple meaning of scripture. Yahweh sends His Son Jesus as a man, to establish His kingdom here on earth. We don't have to complicate this relationship with Greek thought by making God into a substance. This concept is made clear in the New Testament. The Father is referred to as 'God' and Jesus is referred to as 'Lord.'

We know that an idol is nothing at all in the world and that there is no God but one. For even if there are so-called gods, whether in heaven or on earth (as indeed there are many "gods" and many "lords"), yet for us there is but one God, the Father, from whom all things came and for whom we live; and there is but one Lord, Jesus Christ, through whom all things came and through whom we live. (1 Corinthians 8:4-6)

This same relationship is noted once again in Ephesians 4:4-6:

There is one body and one Spirit- just as you were called to one hope when you were called- one Lord, one faith, one baptism; one God and Father of all, who is over all and through all and in all.

We need not deny Jesus as God in terms of a job description.

60

He functions in that role as well. But scripture emphasizes God the Father and the Lord Jesus. The problem with identifying Jesus as God, is that Jesus is God's Son. If we emphasize Jesus as God, instead of Lord, as the New Testament teaches us, we muddy the waters of our understanding.

Seeking God through Logic vs. Faith

A void of Hebraic thought in the early church made room for Greek philosophy to solve the theological issues of the day. In His book, <u>Looking at Philosophy</u>, Donald Palmer concludes that the force behind Greek philosophy is, *"...a certain kind of thinking about the world, a kind of logical analysis that places things in the context of reason and explains them with the pure force of thought."*[3] Among the early church Fathers, logic replaced faith as the primary means of relating to God and understanding the kingdom. The mind became elevated over the heart, and the soul over the spirit.

Palmer goes on to say, *"What was there before philosophy... was 'mythos'- a certain way of thinking that placed the world in the context of supernatural origins."*[4] "Mythos" is the basis of Biblical thought; there is an unexplainable force in the universe that operates outside of reason. This void kept many philosophers in darkness and lost in endless arguments. Few realized this void was the seat for God Himself. Where reason ends, God steps out of the darkness into the light of faith and shines. The philosopher who refuses to step outside this realm of reason to receive truth,

---

[3] Palmer, Donald. *Looking at Philosophy: the Unbearable Heaviness of Philosophy Made Lighter.* Mountain View, CA: Mayfield Pub., 1994. 2.
[4] Ibid.

will never find a way to fill this void.

Truth in the Hebraic mindset is based upon what God has said. God said it, I believe it, that settles it! Truth in the Greek mindset is attained through debated arguments and conclusions. Greeks were often called little children because they were constantly asking, "Why?". The Western mind is always questioning where the Hebraic mind can rest and trust in the unanswered. You can trust an unknown future to a known God! The Greeks called this embracing of the unknown 'mythos'.

'Mythos' provided the early communities with *"..rules that if followed by all, would create the foundations of a genuine community of togetherness- a 'we' and an 'us' instead of a mere conglomeration of individuals who could only say 'I' and 'me'."* [5] Hence, the belief in supernatural origins and foundational truths bring a sense of community. Some things are not in question because they have always *been* from the beginning. On the other hand, 'mythos' if not Biblically based, can create superstition and actions based on fear, because the natural world also operates in the realm of reason. For instance, if I eat too much sugar, I will most likely get cavities. There will be pain in my teeth because I overindulged in what God gave me for pleasure. This is a rational explanation of how sugar deteriorates my teeth. There was no curse, demon, or evil spirit that afflicted me.

Now, because I have pain in my teeth, I will go to a dentist and have my cavities removed. Will I pray for healing? Yes! But,

---

[5] Palmer, Donald. *Looking at Philosophy: the Unbearable Heaviness of Philosophy Made Lighter.* Mountain View, CA: Mayfield Pub., 1994. 2-3.

I will also schedule a dentist appointment while I am waiting for my miracle. Biblical faith understands the operation of reason in the natural realm and respects it. But faith also recognizes that God is not limited by reason either. Faith is the basis for all things and truth is based on what God has said, even when it defies reason.

"Mythos" provided the ancients with a way of explaining why things are. It leaves some questions about our existence reserved for the answer, "Because that is the way it is!" Some questions would remain in this category. Yet the philosopher had no "mythos" category that was reserved for some of life's questions. Everything had to have a rational explanation.

Philosophy is not known for beginning with the assumption of God. Philosophy begins with observation. The Bible never tries to prove the existence of God. It begins with **"In the beginning God."** (Genesis 1:1) If a person's observation is not based on the belief that God **is**, then the Bible refers to that man as a 'fool.' **"The fool says in his heart, "There is no God."** (Psalm 14:1)

Many of the early Christian thinkers were not only theologians, but also philosophers. Without simply accepting that God *is* and Jesus *is*, complicated arguments can arise over non-Biblical issues. Often, their philosophical language frustrates the true emphasis of the gospel from rising to the top.

Philosophical Blunders

Philosophy brought questions to the table that none of the writers of the scriptures had even considered, much less debated amongst each other. Much of the debate in the Early Church resulted in its greater division and opened the door to a millennium of darkness throughout the entire world. I believe early church leaders were reacting to error instead of responding to truth. The main controversy that was brought to the Council of Nicea was between two leading bishops, Athanasius and Arius.

Athanasius prescribed to the Trinity and rightfully despised Arius' view of Christ being a created being. The issue was dealt with but not settled during this council. Both sides fought over how to respond to the person of Christ. As Luther brought the issue of salvation by faith alone to the table over a thousand years later, the Council of Nicea brought the person of Christ to the forefront. The issue, in theological terms is called "Christology"- a study of Christ.

Christology is a theological word that defines your perspective of Christ. For instance, some cults consider Jesus as a mere man or some kind of angel. These would be said to have a low Christology. Others refer to Jesus as God Himself; like Father, like Son. These teachings have a high Christology.

A Biblical Christology puts Jesus at the right hand of His Father, to be worshiped, adored and glorified, as if He was the Father Himself. We must clarify our message; God the Creator sent His Son Jesus to purchase men back to Himself through the blood of His Son Jesus. How we define Jesus Christ divides the cults from the orthodox. If we miss who Jesus is, we miss it altogether. Jesus said, **"If you do not believe that I am the one I claim to be, you will indeed die in your sins." (John 8:24)**

I hope this chapter has clarified some of the language we use as Christians. In fact, clarifying the person of Jesus is my sole purpose for this writing. Satan is most powerful when he can confuse the meaning of our most common words. We lose the heart of what we say when we lose the true meaning of our words.

A quick review of this discussion follows: God is not a name but a title and is most often given to Yahweh, which is God's personal name. Jesus is the Son of Yahweh, the Son of God, who most often claims the title of Lord. Their relationship is best described as that of a Father to a Son. To fully appreciate this picture, one must understand the importance of covenant found throughout the Scriptures. Covenant is a solemn contract, oath, or bond between two parties. The most powerful covenant known to man is that between a father and son. The son is the one who will continue on the dynasty of his father. When a son carries out this solemn duty, there is something beautiful released from heaven to earth.

And now, as surely as the LORD lives—he who has established me securely on the throne of my father David, has founded a dynasty for me as he promised." (1 Kings 2:24)

It is time we restore the covenant language of dynasty back to the New Testament. The next chapter is based upon Psalms chapter two and gives us a clear picture of Jesus and the Father incorporated, acting upon one throne to establish the kingdom on earth.

Reflection

1.   How does the emphasis of "God as great" versus "God as Father" in Islam affect the heart of Muslims throughout the world?

2.   Should we view the word "God" as a substance or as a title?

3.   Many scholars teach that God has many names. The Bible teaches God's personal name is "Yahweh," yet He has many different titles. How does knowing someone's name bring a new dynamic to a relationship?

4.   Do you think that reason has replaced faith as the primary means by which the body of Christ relates to God and understands the kingdom?

5.   What is the importance of the word "Christology?"

chapter 5
Yahweh and Son Incorporated

*P*salm 2 was written by King David about 1,000 years prior to the birth of Jesus. In this very prophetic psalm, David speaks of a mystery soon to be revealed. At the time David wrote this Psalm, the Jews worshipped Yahweh. They followed the laws of Moses and sacrificed according to their traditions. But in David's writings, we begin to discover a plan being revealed that would soon change everything. Yahweh would send a Son, a Messiah, whom He would raise up and place in charge of everything! I like to refer to the Dynasty concept as Yahweh and Son Incorporated.

Yahweh, the Father, says in Psalm 2:1-2:

Why do the nations conspire and the peoples plot in vain? The kings of the earth take their stand against the

LORD and against his Anointed One.

This messianic psalm tells us there will be great opposition against Yahweh and His Anointed One.

Yahweh goes on to say in verse 6, **"I have installed my king on Zion my holy hill. The LORD has set his king in place."** Who is this king? His name is Jesus; He is the 'Anointed One.' This transference of all authority (for a season) from Yahweh to His Anointed One is the "good news," or what we call the gospel.

In verse 7 we read**, "I will proclaim the decree of the LORD. He said to me, "You are my Son."** The anointing is a marking that sets someone apart for a special and unique purpose. Isaiah 61 declares that, **"The Spirit of the LORD is upon me because he has anointed me."** The Spirit of God confirms Sonship because of the anointing.

Anointed Words Bring the Spirit

How does the anointing come? It comes through the Father's *blessing.* And a voice from heaven said, **"This is my Son, whom I love; with him I am well pleased."** (Matthew 3:17) This was the Father empowering His Son.

Words mark a person. Words are carriers of substance from one person to another. God created the blessing to be passed on from father to son. When this blessing is not passed on, the son is not empowered and often struggles to fulfill his destiny.

On the day of his baptism, Jesus was anointed. As I stated

earlier, it was not the baptism that brought the anointing. The anointing came with the *words* spoken from His Heavenly Father. At this very moment, the Holy Spirit was poured out upon Jesus. This is called the Father's Blessing.

One of the greatest messages we can offer people today is the message of the Father's Blessing made available to us through His Son Jesus Christ. We often focus too much on the power of curses, when instead our focus should be on the lack of the Father's blessing.

Our ability to overcome the world is based upon the acknowledgment of Jesus as God's Son. **"Who is it that overcomes the world? Only he who believes that Jesus is the Son of God."** (1 John 5:5) God is proud to release His authority in heaven and earth to His Son.

When the Lord says**, "You are my Son. Today I have become your father,"** in Psalm 2:7, many question the preexistence of the Son. The word in the Hebrew language is often translated begotten. We hear this word in the King James Version of John 3:16:

For God so loved the world that He gave his only begotten son that whosoever believes in Him should not perish but have everlasting life.

The LORD says the Son, "I have begotten you- I have given you birth," in reference to Him becoming flesh and being born into this world. **"The Word became flesh and made his dwelling among us."** (John 1:14)

This refers to the birth of Jesus not to God Himself. *God did not become flesh.* God's Son became flesh to point us back to the Father.

The word *begotten* in the Greek is the word *monogenes,* which means "unique, one of a kind, one and only, precious, beloved."[1] Jesus' relationship to the Father is a one of a kind relationship. Jesus is not claiming to be God, but God's Son. This is the one and only relationship that is occupied by Jesus Himself and no other.

Jesus is the Prince

Jesus assumes the position of Prince of Peace. During the season when we celebrate the birth of Jesus, we often hear Isaiah 9:6 quoted: **"For to us a child is born, to us a son is given, and the government will be on his shoulders."** The remainder of the verse in most Christian translations says: **"And he will be called Wonderful Counselor, Mighty God, Everlasting Father, Prince of Peace."** Is Jesus to take the title as the Mighty God and the Everlasting Father?

According to the Complete Jewish Bible, the translation of Isaiah 9:6 is as follows:

For a child has been born to us, a son given to us and the authority is upon his shoulder and the wondrous Advisor,

---

[1] Zodhiates, Spiros, and John R. Kohlenberger. *The Hebrew-Greek Key Study Bible: New International Version.* Chattanooga, TN: AMG Pub., 1996. 1652.

the mighty God, the everlasting Father called his name 'The Prince of Peace.' [2]

In the 6th century A.D., the Hebrew of the Old Testament adopted vowel markings to help with the pronunciation of the Scriptures. The modification of "he called" instead "he will be called" is determined by the vowel markings and can be translated either way. I believe the Complete Jewish Bible translation is more accurate and makes more sense in light of the rest of Scripture.

Jesus assumes this position, as the Prince, and is the only access point to the Father. That is why Jesus says, **"No one comes to the Father except through me."** (John 14:6) Psalms chapter two points to the Son as the place of refuge from destruction.

Therefore kings of the earth be wise be warned you rulers of the earth. Serve the lord with fear and rejoice with trembling. Kiss the Son lest he be angry and you be destroyed in your way. Blessed are those who take refuge in Him. (Psalm 2:11-12)

Notice how Yahweh says of Jesus **"kiss the Son,"** or you will be destroyed. It is a warning to all who say, "I worship God" but fail to honor the Son. We must proclaim the news that God has a Son and now everything in this world and the world to come depends upon our response to Him.

---

[2] "Yeshayahu - Chapter 9 - Tanakh Online - Torah - Bible." Judaism, Torah and Jewish Info - Chabad Lubavitch. Web. 17 Mar. 2011.
<http://www.chabad.org/library/bible_cdo/aid/15940/showrashi/true>.

Even in the English language, God has placed an interesting pun. Our world is totally dependent upon the sun. Without the sun shining, we would perish. In the same way, we are dependent on the Son for life. Without Him, we will perish.

The promise of Psalm 2 says, **"Blessed are all those who take refuge in him."** This refers to those who take refuge and put their trust in Jesus Christ. Jesus is His name and Christ or Messiah is His job description. Jesus is the Anointed One and also the Son, the one we must kiss and serve, the one seated at the right hand of his Father. The Father has released the kingdom of God upon the Son whom He loves. In Luke 22:29, Jesus says, **"And I confer on you a kingdom just as my father conferred one on me."** Jesus now lives in us by the Spirit and we are completing the work of kingdom for the Father!

So who does Jesus claim to be? In our culture we make it our emphasis to say, "Jesus is God." However, this claim is never made in the Scriptures! Translators have tried to work the texts to imply this message, but Jesus continually emphasizes that He is not 'another God.' He is in covenant with the Father and now rules and continues His Father's dynasty as the Anointed One or Messiah. We are not to think any less of Jesus because we do not give Him the title as "God." We are to treat Him in the same manner as the Father.

The Word was with God

The Prince of Heaven ascends to the throne of His Father. This is a picture of a Son who is with His Father on the throne. Early theologians feared Jesus would not be treated with the same authority as God Himself and felt it necessary to emphasize the idea that "Jesus is God." The idea of a

'Godhead' or 'Trinity,' came into being to address the idea of Jesus "as God" and "with God" as if through some mysterious transformation. John opens his gospel with these words:

In the beginning was the Word, and the Word was with God, and the Word was God. He was with God in the beginning. (John 1:1-2)

John highlights the Word being with God in these two verses. But the translation above says that the "Word was God." The Greek translation lacks of a definite article in regards to the Word. It literally says the Word was a God.

Most translators ignore the lack of the definite article because it conveys a message that Jesus was 'a god' and the Father was 'the God.' I would rather err on the side of viewing Christ as God, than viewing Him as anything less. My concern would be to say that Christ is the Father, or some kind of being that transforms God into something different than Yahweh Himself. I prefer the following translation from the New English Bible:

When all things began, the Word already was. The Word dwelt with God, and what God was, the Word was.[3]

Everything that God is, Jesus is! The Son assumes every quality that the Father exhibits. I believe that the Gospel of John began with this statement in order to clarify who Jesus

---

[3] "The New Testament." The New English Bible: The Apocrypha. Oxford [u.a.: University, 1970. 110. Print.

was. The Word is the Son of God who became flesh so that He could take up our sin and set us free to have a relationship with the Father. Jesus was with God for that very purpose and accomplished His Father's desires in obedience.

Jesus Brings Us Into Covenant

"The Word became flesh and made his dwelling among us." (John 1:14)   Jesus became flesh and dwelt among us to restore us back into fellowship with the Father. There was a person in our fellowship recently who was in the process of donating one of their kidneys to a relative who was on dialysis. This procedure could not take place until the doctors were assured that the donor organ would be a match for the recipient.

In a similar manner, Jesus became a man so that He would be a match for all humanity. Yet mankind needs much more than a kidney transplant. The cross was the procedure in which He gave up His heart so we might get a new one. Jesus endured the heart transplant to offer all mankind life. This is what it means to be 'born again'.

Jesus is not only Lord of all, but also takes the role as the One who brings us into the covenant family of God. He brings us into relationship with the Father because He is the beloved Son of God. The Lord reminded me of this vivid truth in a story I heard years ago.

Back in the 1800's in San Francisco, there were two brothers who moved into a violent area. The younger brother decided to get involved with a bunch of thugs and in time ended up in a knife fight in which he murdered another man. As he fled the scene, he ran into his house and up into his room, throwing his bloody clothes on the floor and hiding in the closet.

The next thing he heard was someone coming up the stairs, then someone breaking down the door, and then commotion, followed by total silence. After a few moments, he came out of the closet, only to realize that his big brother had put on his blood-soaked shirt and was taken away by the police to be put to death for his younger brother's crime.

Jesus is the older brother in this story who loved us so much that He was willing to give His life for us. He became flesh, so that He could put on our bloody clothes and be a big brother to us. Our guilt and shame had to be paid for by one like Adam.

For since death came through a man, the resurrection of the dead comes also through a man. For as in Adam all die, so in Christ all will be made alive. (1 Corinthians 15:21-22)

God is Father to us because Jesus married us and is now teaching us how to be part of the family. Jesus came to show us how a son ought to relate to a father. But because of Adam's sin, we needed a redeemer to come and pay the price for our covenant violations. These covenant violations are called curses. **"Christ redeemed us from the curse of the law by becoming a curse for us, for it is written: "Cursed is everyone who is hung on a tree."** (Galatians 3:13)

When Jesus was hung on the tree, which was His crucifixion, He took our punishment upon Himself. Jesus fully satisfied God's wrath toward man because he made Himself obedient to the cross for you and I. Jesus had to look like Adam to be punished for Adam. Jesus had to be able to fit into Adam's blood stained T-shirt, taking on the role of the older brother. Paul referred to Jesus as the 'last Adam', who came in the image of Adam and also the image of God.

75

So it is written: "The first man Adam became a living being;" the last Adam, a life-giving spirit. The spiritual did not come first, but the natural, and after that the spiritual. The first man was of the dust of the earth, the second man from heaven. As was the earthly man, so are those who are of the earth; and as is the man from heaven, so also are those who are of heaven. And just as we have borne the likeness of the earthly man, so shall we bear the likeness of the man from heaven. (1 Corinthians 15:45-49)

This principle is referred to as the first-fruits principle. God established the feast of first-fruits to teach us a spiritual principle. Jewish tradition tells us that on the day of Passover, the priest would go into the field and cut down the first-fruits portion of the harvest. Passover is the feast day on which Jesus was crucified. Once the first-fruits portion was cut down on the day of Passover, it would lie there until the day after the Sabbath. The feast of first-fruits is described in Leviticus 23.

The LORD said to Moses, "Speak to the Israelites and say to them: When you enter the land I am going to give you and you reap its harvest, bring to the priest a sheaf of the first grain you harvest. He is to wave the sheaf before the LORD so it will be accepted on your behalf; the priest is to wave it on the day after the Sabbath." (Leviticus 23:9-11)

Now here is the picture: Christ was cut down on Passover Day and lay in the tomb three days and three nights, only to be raised up on the day after the Sabbath. Paul describes Christ this way: "But Christ has indeed been raised from the dead, the first-fruits of those who have fallen asleep" (1 Corinthians 15:20).

Imagery is the best way to fully understand truth and that is why God chose to use simple, ordinary life to express how He operates. Imagine watching the actions of this priest, cutting down a stalk of barley and letting it lie in the field for three days. Then on the third day, the priest raises up the sheaf and waving it before the LORD, declaring it to be the first-fruits of the entire harvest. Jesus is the first-fruit offering declaring the rest of the harvest holy as well. This is a kingdom principle.

If the part of the dough offered as firstfruits is holy, then the whole batch is holy; if the root is holy, so are the branches. Here the principle of the first-fruits is established. (Romans 11:16)

Jesus offered His life up for us as an offering to God and He was accepted as a pleasing, acceptable sacrifice sent for you and me.

There is a reason we must get specific when it relates to theology. We must emphasize what Jesus emphasized and what the Word teaches. Jesus said that eternal life is in knowing the only true God and whom He sent. **"Now this is eternal life: that they may know you, the only true God, and Jesus Christ, whom you have sent."** (John 17:3)

As much as I must emphasize that Jesus is not the Most High God, rather He is the son of Yahweh; I must also emphasize that Jesus is everything Yahweh ever was. Jesus is not limited by time, space or power. He is present everywhere through the Holy Spirit!

The kingdom of God is both Yahweh and Son incorporated. The Father and Son are one in covenant. The

77

next chapter will redefine our understanding of the word 'one' and relate its meaning back to its roots in the Hebraic language.

Reflection

1. God the Father passed on His blessing to His Son Jesus. What can we do to make this model of passing on the blessing, father to son, prominent in our culture?

2. Viewing Jesus as a Prince who ascends into power is the message of Psalm 2. How do you think early Jews understood this Psalm?

3. How would you communicate the message, "Kiss the Son?"

4. Can you see yourself in the story as the younger brother guilty of murder? How does the picture of Jesus as our caring older brother impact you?

5. The paradigm shift of 'Yahweh and Son Incorporated' places a different emphasis over traditional theology. How does this concept play out on a day-to-day basis?

chapter six
One In Covenant

With a focus on Jewish and Muslim evangelism, what is the best strategy to reach them? They believe in God, but not in His Son Jesus. Our goal is to introduce them to the One who can bring them to the Father. The only way that the kingdom can be released, is through the name of Jesus and with the power of this conviction: **"I am not ashamed of the gospel because it is the power of God unto salvation."** (Romans 1:16) We should not try to convince the Muslim or the Jew with a better argument, but instead with more power. Paul said, **"For the kingdom of God is not a matter of talk, but of power."** (1 Corinthians 4:20)

I remember leading worship at a meeting and while we were worshipping, and I began to see in the Spirit people in bondage, wrapped in chains. These chains, however, had a combination lock, not with numbers, but with letters of the alphabet. Once the person came forward, I saw myself lining up the five slots with the letters J-E-S-U-S. Every chain was broken when the name of Jesus was used.

The world needs an encounter with Jesus! The church has a mandate to present the truth with simplicity and power. Heaven's dynasty is continued on earth through the Son of God. The Jews have rejected Christianity for centuries but many secretly admired Jesus.

This chapter will present the many logical and legitimate reasons why many Jews have rejected Christianity. Christians have failed in word and deed when dealing with the Jew. Looking back at the Crusades and the Holocaust, we should be aware that the Jews have experienced persecution and death at the hands of Christians. Let's take a look at our history.

Jewish Rejection of Christianity

Throughout history, the Jew was often given only one option; remain a Jew or become a Christian. Most Jewish people cannot imagine rejecting their own identity, as this would also mean rejecting their God. Given this model, they are right to stay Jewish! The Christian establishment should have never suggested that by becoming a follower of Jesus, you were no longer Jewish. Jesus Himself was Jewish!

We must seek to remove all barriers that have hindered the Jews from receiving Jesus as the Messiah. Yet many of the basic doctrines of Christianity, when seen through scaled eyes, are completely opposite of what is ingrained into the Jewish mind. Jesus has to be the Jewish Messiah, or He cannot be anyone's

Messiah.

The New Testament declares Jesus to be Lord, but not specifically God. Yahweh is God: He always was and always will be. This is where we must address Trinitarian language. Doctrines that cause us to lose our focus on the Father and Son relationship between Yahweh and Jesus have only served to confuse many. When we stray from the Bible in our language, we will lose favor with the people of the book; the Jews.

The 'Shema'

The most important verse in the Bible to the Jew is Deuteronomy 6:4, **"Hear O Israel, the LORD is God, the LORD is one."** This verse in the Hebrew language is so important, it has a title: 'The Shema'. *Shema* in Hebrew means, "to hear and obey." 'The Shema' is one of the key scriptures theologians discuss when developing the person of God and His Son Jesus. This scripture is to the Jew what John 3:16 is to the Christian.

Famous Jews throughout history have spoken the 'Shema' in their last breath. It was a defiant cry that made them different from pantheistic religions that surrounded them. According to Josephus, Abraham, *"...was the first that ventured to publish this notion, that there was but One God."*[1] Viewing God as 'one' for the Jew is a sacred duty.

---

[1] Josephus, Flavius, and William Whiston. *The Live of Flavius Josephus. Antiquities of the Jews : 1-8*. Vol. 1. Philadelphia, PA: Lippincott, Grambo and, 1850. 23.

Rabbis throughout the centuries have emphasized the singularity of God in the 'Shema.' I believe the real Biblical emphasis is not His singularity, but rather His desire for covenant. 'One' in Hebraic thought denotes being together in covenant. We must keep this in mind when forming our theology.

The word for 'one' in 'the Shema' is the Hebrew word *echad*. It means, "united, one, alike, alone, altogether." 'The Shema' is placed in the context of the Ten Commandments (or words) from Yahweh to His people. Following this verse is the scripture urging them to **"Love the LORD your God with all your heart, with all your soul, with all your mind, and with all your strength."** (vs.5)

Echad is used to signify a union or a joining together in covenant. When 'one' is referred to in relationships, it points to a covenant, not a number. Yahweh was telling His people that He is a covenant making God, not that He was singular! This is why 'the Shema' is found right in the midst of Yahweh's covenant promise.

Take for instance the following scripture in Genesis regarding man and woman becoming *echad*. **"For this reason a man will leave his father and mother and be united to his wife, and they will become *one* flesh."** (Genesis 2:24) When I got married, I became one flesh with my wife, yet we did not cease to exist as individuals. We share my last name, but we continue as separate people. We did not join our first names together to metamorphous into some indefinable mass. *Echad* meant we became one in covenant.

The first sentence in Genesis 1:1 states, **"...God created..."** The Hebrew noun *Elohim* is plural, but the verb for create, *bara*, is singular. The plural *Elohim* leaves many to believe that God is hinting that He is more than one. However there are other explanations for the use of *Elohim* (i.e. God plural) in the Scriptures. For example, plurality in the Hebrew language is sometimes used "to emphasize or to magnify." The grammar of ancient languages does not always follow the rules of the English language.

Not the Number One

The 'oneness of God' is an issue that must be clarified for the Jewish people. Jesus did not come to promote pantheism. He came to do the will of the One God. It was Jesus Himself who quoted Deuteronomy 6:4-5 when asked what was the most important of all commandments. He would not break the commandment that He called most important. As followers of Christ, we too, must seek to find the true meaning of 'the Shema.'

Jesus' relationship to the Father is that of *echad-* one in covenant. We do not need to justify "the Shema" in the New Testament by creating a new doctrine that combines them together into one substance. Jesus, in covenant with Yahweh, fulfills his duty as a Son. This is how Jesus prays:

My prayer is not for them alone. I pray also for those who will believe in me through their message, that all of them may be one, Father, just as you are in me and I am in you. May they also be in us so that the world may believe that you have sent me. I have given them the glory that you gave me, that they may be one as we are one: I in them and you in me. May they be brought to complete unity to let the world know that you sent me and have loved them even as you have loved me. (John 17:20-23)

83

Jesus prayed that we may be one as He and the Father are one; one in covenant together. I believe early Church Fathers sought to defend the oneness of God as stated in 'the Shema', but lacked the Hebraic understanding of what 'the Shema' really meant. Jesus was not to be added to God, but literally to *be* the Son who ascended to the throne of His Father.

I read the Scriptures seeking to understand not only what is said, but also what is not said. As I read the writings of the first Christians, we find Jesus the Son, and God the Father. Later writings began to complicate the language by adding words like divinity, Trinity and Godhead, in hopes of better defining who God is. Why not just use the simple devotional language that was already provided in the New Testament?

No doubt the early church had its problems. The person of Christ was often put into question. If God was 'one' and Jesus was more than an angel and definitely more than a man, how could they explain this new dynamic without becoming polytheists? (a person worshipping two or more gods)

The Bible declares that there is only one God and His name is Yahweh. The Bible also declares that God has a Son and His name is Jesus. The Bible also declares that there is only one throne on which the Father and Son sit, and upon this throne, the kingdom of God will be established upon the earth.

Yahweh's dynasty is being established through His Son. Jesus conquered the grave and now sits in the highest place at the right hand of the Father. Jesus sits upon the throne, releasing the kingdom of God upon earth, and the Spirit of God is poured out upon all who declare Jesus Christ is Lord.

84

The Preeminence of Jesus

Now that Jesus is ruling, there is a clear focus we must place on the name of Jesus. Because the Son is seated at the right hand of the Father and, **"All authority in Heaven and Earth has been given to him..."** (Matt 28:20), we must lead people to Him, so they can have access to the Father. In John 14:6, Jesus said, **"I am the way and the truth and the life. No one comes to the Father except through me."** (John 14:6)

I graduated from a Messianic Bible School that encouraged me to think like the early disciples- from a Jewish perspective. One day I decided to read through the book of Acts to discover what their message was then, versus what our message has become today. The Westernized Christian message is "Jesus is God." Yet, the early church never preached this message. Their message was, "Jesus is Lord." Acts 9:20 says, **"Saul spent several days with the disciples in Damascus. At once he began to preach in the synagogues that Jesus is the Son of God."**

What is the difference you might ask? The difference is subtle, but very important. By declaring that Jesus is God, we are actually saying that Jesus is the Father, or Jesus is Yahweh. Jesus specifically referred to himself as the Son of God. Jesus says of Himself under oath:

Then the high priest stood up and said to Jesus, "Are you not going to answer? What is this testimony that these men are bringing against you?" But Jesus remained silent. The high priest said to him, "I charge you under oath by the living God: Tell us if you are the Christ, the Son of God." "Yes, it is as you say," Jesus replied. "But I say to all of you: In the future you will see the Son of Man

85

sitting at the right hand of the Mighty One and coming on the clouds of heaven." (Matthew 26:62-64)

Here we have a statement made under oath. At this point Jesus should have said, according to the Creeds, "I am the Second Part of the Godhead!"

John 3:16 does not say, "For God so loved the world, that He gave up the second part of the Godhead, that whosoever believes in Him shall not perish but have everlasting life." The gospel says that God gave up His Son. How much easier is it to relate to this message: a Father who loves His Son, and gives Him up for us, and the Son willingly giving up His life so that we might be saved?

Is God a Three-Part Being?

Many believe God has revealed himself as a three part being, just like we have a body, a soul and a spirit. In the same way, God the Father is said to be the mind, Jesus the body and the Holy Spirit is the spirit.

Most of us have been taught that 'God is in Three Persons,' each separate yet still one. But let's face it: few really understand the Trinity. It is a complicated thought process that many of us just receive by faith. We have been taught to accept this concept without reservation, and like obedient Christians, we have been trying to apply it. We feel obligated to accept what we do not understand, without considering that maybe we have overcomplicated things!

For the past 1700 years, the Trinity has served the church as a model that esteems Jesus Christ to the highest place of honor.

The concept of God in three persons- Christ being one of them- keeps Christ from being looked upon as a created being, or from being treated any differently from the Father. The Trinity upholds these vital truths for every Christian.

But I believe God has a heart of simplicity. When Jesus walked the earth, He used everyday ideas that simple people like you and me could grasp. The Trinity, on the other hand, is probably the greatest and most influential intellectual masterpiece in the history of Christianity. The model of the Triune God, is an observation from a philosophical and scientific point of view that requires great intellect. The result leads us to relegate the concept of the Trinity to a mystery to be accepted by faith.

My journey has compelled me to define a model, with the relational emphasis that is obvious to all who read. This Biblical model emphasizes not Three in One, but a Father and Son Dynasty, where the Son rules the kingdom, seated on His Father's throne.

Christians have used many analogies from nature to teach God as a three-part being. I used to teach that God is like water: one substance but in three separate states. Water can be a steam, a liquid, or a solid chunk of ice, each state dependent upon the temperature. Even light has a three part dynamic, as does music. But these examples from nature fail to express the meaningful relationship between a Father and a Son.

Rethinking this argument, I have had to ask the question, *"Have the Scriptures ever put forth this argument? Did Jesus teach his disciples that He flowed with the Father and the Spirit like water, steam and ice?"* Water is an example of one substance in three parts, but I find nowhere in Scripture that we are to view God as we

87

view water.

I have been in different countries and have seen firsthand the importance of emphasizing the heart of Father God to His people. When I explain the chemical make-up of water, no one is moved to tears. Hearts are not touched over inanimate objects. But when I explain the Father's heart from the story of the prodigal son, people are moved. Everyone can relate to the joy or pain that comes from either the love, or lack of love from a father.

The very center of our belief should lie in the idea of covenant relationship, not in science and substance. God is not a substance to be examined; He is Father. The proclamation of a loving Father and His Faithful Son must be the true core of our message.

In my opinion, 'Godhead' language not only lacks a relational message, but also has most often been presented as a mystery. I believe the Father has lovingly placed around us earthly patterns to understand Him so that we can approach Him accordingly. He does not want us to be unclear about who He is and how we can relate to Him and His Son.

Many Christians have great difficulty approaching God because they have relational problems with their earthly father. My own struggle came out of being raised in an alcoholic home. My view of my earthly father was one who was present but not actively involved.

In my prayer times, my heart knew God was present, but I did not believe He would become actively involved with me. Whenever I prayed alone this feeling would haunt me. I recognized the connection between how I perceived my earthly father and how I related to my Heavenly Father.

One day as I was praying, this haunting feeling came over me again. As I was in that place, the Father showed me in the Spirit a lump of clay and He asked me, "Does the potter have the final image in mind before he begins working on the lump?" Something happened in my heart that day! I no longer needed others to pray with to have breakthrough. He said to me, "I AM the potter and you are the clay! I have exactly in mind what you are going to become. Every time I touch you and mold you, it is for a purpose. I have a plan for you and I am actively shaping you into the image of my Son Jesus." The prophet Isaiah said:

Yet, O LORD, you are our Father. We are the clay, you are the potter; we are all the work of your hand. (Isaiah 64:8)

Have you considered the impact your earthly father has had upon your perspective of your Heavenly Father? Take a moment and ponder that thought. Forgive your father and honor him before God. I have seen countless times that once this relationship is made right, your connection with God will be renewed. Honoring earthly fathers and mothers is one of the most important commands given to us to follow.

"Honor your father and mother'—which is the first commandment with a promise— 'that it may go well with you and that you may enjoy long life on the earth." (Ephesians 6:2-3)

Honor releases us into a long life! We must honor those God calls us to honor. When we honor Jesus, we are honoring the Father. Honoring Jesus brings pleasure to the Father and gives us access to enjoy a long life.

Moreover, the Father judges no one, but has entrusted all judgment to the Son, that all may honor the Son just as they honor the Father. (John 5:22)

Consider how many people in the world today desire to honor God with their lives, but have a problem with Jesus. May *all* honor the Son! The Father is shouting to the world about Jesus, **"This is my Son, whom I love. Listen to him!"** (Mark 9:7)

In theological terms, orthodoxy is based upon the person of Jesus Christ. In simple terms, we must treat Him in the same way we treat the Father. I believe God is restoring the idea of covenant relationships back to the body of Christ. If we are in covenant with Him, then we are 'one.' Jesus even pointed to 'the Shema' as the most important verse to remember. **"'The most important one,' answered Jesus, 'is this: Hear, O Israel, the Lord our God, the Lord is one.'"** (Mark 12:29)

A Covenant Emphasis

As we understand that 'one' is not in reference to a number, but rather to a covenantal relationship, we begin to feel the heartbeat of the gospel. Yahweh has offered a covenant relationship to the whole world through His Son Jesus. Those who honor Jesus, and make Him Lord, enter into covenant with God Himself.

For this reason Christ is the mediator of a new covenant, that those who are called may receive the promised

eternal inheritance-now that he has died as a ransom to set them free from the sins committed under the first covenant. (Hebrews 9:15)

Ancients would use the phrase 'cutting covenant.' The Hebrew word that is used alongside the word covenant is the word *karath*. This word implies "the cutting of the flesh in some way so that blood would flow out."[2] Consider what occurred when God made a covenant with Abraham. Abraham fell into a trance and the LORD entered into covenant with him. Here is what happened:

When the sun had set and darkness had fallen, a smoking firepot with a blazing torch appeared and passed between the pieces. On that day the LORD made a covenant with Abram. (Genesis 15:17-18)

When the ancients 'cut' covenant, the common practice was to cut an animal in two, and each member of the covenant would walk between the carcasses declaring, "May the same fate happen to me if I ever violate the terms of this agreement with you!" Yet when God made covenant with Abraham, we do not see him walking between the pieces. God established the covenant while Abraham was in a trance. He rested while the LORD made the covenant.

Our covenant with God is no different in that Jesus did the work for us while we were not even seeking Him. Jesus not only brought us into covenant relationship with the Father, but

---

[2] Zodhiates, Spiros, and John R. Kohlenberger. *The Hebrew-Greek Key Study Bible: New International Version*. Chattanooga, TN: AMG Pub., 1996. 1524.

He also became the 'torn one' because of our covenantal violations. Jesus took the punishment for us.

But he was pierced for our transgressions, he was crushed for our iniquities; the punishment that brought us peace was upon him, and by his wounds we are healed. (Isaiah 53:5)

Imagine the impact of making covenant with another party. Once the covenant was cut, both parties would walk in greater confidence throughout life, knowing they were not alone. Being in covenant means being 'one' in heart with each other.

To the ancients, every act was viewed as righteous or unrighteous, according to ones loyalty to the covenant. Sadly today, most of us have lost the deep understanding of covenant. We have no clue that we are living such empty lives because we lack covenant relationships. The entire breakdown of our culture is directly tied to this missing element!

One interesting dynamic in the Hebrew language was that the word 'friend' only applied to those with whom you were in covenant.[3] With this concept in mind, we can read John 15 in a new light:

Greater love has no one than this, that he lay down his life for his friends. You are my friends if you do what I

---

[3] Intrater, Keith. *Covenant Relationships: a More Excellent Way : a Handbook for Integrity and Loyalty in the Body of Christ.* Shippensburg, PA: Destiny Image, 1989. Print.

command. I no longer call you servants, because a servant does not know his master's business. Instead, I have called you friends, for everything that I learned from my Father I have made known to you. You did not choose me, but I chose you and appointed you to go and bear fruit- fruit that will last. Then the Father will give you whatever you ask in my name. This is my command: Love each other. (John 15:13-17)

Jesus has called us into covenant with the Father through His broken body and through His own blood. This covenant makes us 'one' with God. His body on earth is also, one in Christ; one not emphasizing a number, but emphasizing the sense of relationship that covenant provides.

In the next chapter, we will take a closer look at Jesus' role as the Son of God; the One showing us the way to the Father.

Reflection

1. What is 'the Shema' and how did this verse influence Jewish response to Jesus as God's Son?
2. The word *echad* is the word one in Hebrew. Describe the connection between God being *echad* and a man and wife being *echad*.
3. Most theology emphasizes the idea that "Jesus is God." Is this the most accurate message of the New Testament?
4. When we use examples from nature to describe God as a threefold being, is there a danger in missing the relational message of a Father and a Son?
5. How should we communicate the meaning of the word *one* from the Scriptures with a relational versus a mathematical perspective?

chapter seven
Jesus, Son of God

*I*n space travel, your trajectory will determine your destination. A small shift in trajectory will put you in a completely different place. In my understanding of Church history, the trajectory was shifted off course because of a lack of Jewish perspective in our theology. I find that most Christian theology lacks an emphasis on relationship. The theology may be correct, but all truth is not equal. Some truth carries more weight. Our understanding of covenant relationship must not be overlooked in our consideration of theological truth.

Jesus walked, ate, and lived life with the disciples for three years. Imagine them one night after a day of ministry in Caesarea Philippi sitting around a campfire. Jesus looks at the men that surround Him and asks this question, **"Who do people say the Son of Man is?"** James may have replied, **"They think you are John the Baptist!"** John states, **"Most** think you are Elijah!" Andrew then speaks up and says, "**You are Jeremiah or one of the prophets.**" The Lord's gaze then falls upon Peter and He asks, "**But what about you? Who do you say I am?**"

Throughout the centuries, people all over the world have had to answer this same question. And just like in the days of Jesus, there were many different opinions about who Jesus was. Jesus looked to Simon to hear what was in his heart.

Simon Peter answered, "You are the Christ, the Son of the living God." Jesus replied, "Blessed are you, Simon son of Jonah, for this was not revealed to you by man, but by my Father in heaven." (Matthew 16:13-17)

Peter answered correctly and received the revelation that Jesus was the Christ, the Son of the living God. Jesus did not correct Peter at this point and say, "No, that is incorrect. I am fully God and also fully man, and I exist as part of a Godhead." This revelation of Jesus as the Son of the living God comes directly from the Father in heaven. As a Son, Jesus is bringing all who receive Him into covenant with the Father.

Jesus takes Office

Let me give you an example from history. John Adams was the second president of the United States and his son, John Quincy, served as president four terms later. Imagine you had an opportunity to talk to John Quincy about his father. His praise and adoration of his father would be no surprise. However, as a son of a president, he is no less a president than his father was.

In a similar manner, Jesus assumes the 'God' position in this era, though we should refer to Him as 'Lord' to signify the difference. We do not have to make Jesus part of Yahweh in some kind of mysterious oneness to be Biblical. But like John Quincy Adams in his presidency, we must honor the position to which the son has ascended and treat him no differently than we would treat his father. Jesus told His disciples in John 14:28:

You heard me say, "I am going away and I am coming back to you." If you loved me, you would be glad that I am going to the Father, for the Father is greater than I.

Jesus, like every good Son, adored His Father and looked up to Him. God Himself, like every good Father, proudly declares of His Son to all, **"This is my Son, whom I love. Listen to him!"** (Mark 9:7)

Initially, when I first began to question the concept of a 'Godhead' or 'Trinity', I felt very uneasy. *I was afraid that Jesus would in some way be dishonored.* I had been taught to accept the concept of God in three persons, and, like a 'good' Christian, attempted to live it out. Yet the more I studied and the more I read the Bible, I discovered there was no need to define God outside the concept of dynasty. The Prince of Peace, Jesus, fully assumes His role as King, and we honor Him as we honor the Father. In my opinion, I have not found the need to teach a 'Trinity' or 'Godhead' to satisfy the message of Jesus. Yet, many qualified scholars feel this language is necessary to fully relay what the Bible says about God.

Many also use the statement that Jesus was 'fully God and fully man.' You will never read this statement in Scripture. Jesus would have never said that He was 'fully God.' He did not consider equality with God something to be grasped. Jesus'

97

Father is 'fully God' and Jesus is 'fully the Son of God.' But He also came as a man in humility, as Paul writes:

Who, being in very nature God, did not consider equality with God something to be grasped, but made himself nothing, taking the very nature of a servant, being made in human likeness. (Philippians 2:6-7)

When the scripture refers to the 'very nature' of God, it means that Jesus is acting in the *position* of God, but not that He *becomes* Yahweh. Jesus also takes the 'very nature of a servant,' meaning He took the lowly position of a slave. His nature was not altered, but merely the way in which He behaved in His environment.

And being found in appearance as a man, he humbled himself and became obedient to death— even death on a cross! Therefore God exalted him to the highest place and gave him the name that is above every name, that at the name of Jesus every knee should bow, in heaven and on earth and under the earth, and every tongue confess that Jesus Christ is Lord, to the glory of God the Father. (Philippians 2:8-11)

The New Testament makes a clear distinction between God the Father and the Lord Jesus Christ. When we use theology to squeeze the Father and Son together, then adding the Holy Spirit as well, I think we lose a necessary distinction that the Bible clearly makes. There is one God; Yahweh, and one Lord; Jesus, one dynasty, and a Father and a Son who are establishing the kingdom of heaven on earth.

Jewish Perspective of God

From a Jewish standpoint, Yahweh as 'Godhead' seems to be a foreign concept. The danger, in my opinion, of accepting a 'Godhead', is this doctrine would be pointing the Jew to a different God other than Yahweh. The Jew has a clear mandate in the Torah (1ˢᵗ five books of the Old Testament) to reject anyone that leads him or her to another God:

If your very own brother, or your son or daughter, or the wife you love, or your closest friend secretly entices you, saying, "Let us go and worship other gods" (gods that neither you nor your fathers have known, gods of the peoples around you, whether near or far, from one end of the land to the other), do not yield to him or listen to him. Show him no pity. Do not spare him or shield him. You must certainly put him to death. (Deuteronomy 13:6-9)

Consider the consequences of referring to Jesus as 'God'. To the Jew, He would be another god that their fathers had never known. Even though Jesus performed miracles, signs and wonders, they must remain faithful to the Old Testament by *not* listening to His message, since they perceived He was *not* pointing to Yahweh. In fact, the crucifixion would have been justified by the Jewish leadership if Jesus claimed to be God.

If a prophet, or one who foretells by dreams, appears among you and announces to you a miraculous sign or wonder, and if the sign or wonder of which he has spoken takes place, and he says, "Let us follow other gods" (gods you have not known) "and let us worship them," you must not listen to the words of that prophet or dreamer. The LORD your God is testing you to find out whether you love him with all your heart and with all your soul. It

99

is the **LORD** your God you must follow, and him you must revere. Keep his commands and obey him; serve him and hold fast to him. That prophet or dreamer must be put to death, because he preached rebellion against the **LORD** your God, who brought you out of Egypt and redeemed you from the land of slavery; he has tried to turn you from the way the **LORD** your God commanded you to follow. You must purge the evil from among you. (Deuteronomy 13:1-5)

If Jesus claimed to be God Himself, or the second part of the Godhead, the Jews would have been justified in killing Him for His claims. That is why Jesus emphasized His devotion to Yahweh, the God the Israel. When His disciples returned from casting out demons, Jesus responded:

At that time Jesus, full of joy through the Holy Spirit, said, "I praise you, Father, Lord of heaven and earth, because you have hidden these things from the wise and learned, and revealed them to little children. Yes, Father, for this was your good pleasure." (Luke 10:21)

Jesus praised His Father! He didn't praise Himself! He directed worship back to His Father. Even though the Gospels are full of accounts of Jesus performing miraculous signs and wonders, it is unscriptural to follow Him or anyone *for that reason alone.* Jesus however proves He is not a false prophet, because He never encourages people to follow other gods. Jesus always points people back to Yahweh. He said, **"Do not think that I have come to abolish the Law or the Prophets: I have not come to abolish them but to fulfill them."** (Mt. 5:17) He never claimed to point people to a 'Godhead' or 'Trinity' that He was part of: Jesus always pointed them back to His Father.

I remember watching a documentary once produced by a Jewish man. As he was talking to a professor of religion, he made a statement that basically summarized his understanding of the three major religions: "Jews worship Yahweh, Muslims worship Allah, and Christians worship the Triune God- the Trinity." As he made this comment, I realized the powerful connection we could make with the Jews by saying, "Christians worship Yahweh and Son." To the Jew, the Trinity is foreign.

God Has a Son

God has a Son and the Father has made Him the source of eternal life to all who would follow Him. Jesus' desire was in leading everyone back to the Father. He said to the Jews:

My sheep listen to my voice; I know them, and they follow me. I give them eternal life, and they shall never perish; no one can snatch them out of my hand. My Father, who has given them to me, is greater than all; no one can snatch them out of my Father's hand. I and the Father are one. (John 10:27-30)

When Jesus says, **"I and the Father are one,"** He is not making a mathematical statement. Remember that the word 'one' from a Hebraic standpoint means, 'in covenant together'. Jesus was not claiming to be part of Godhead, but was simply declaring He was in covenant with Yahweh Himself. Note the reaction of the Jews:

Again the Jews picked up stones to stone him, but Jesus said to them, "I have shown you many great miracles from the Father. For which of these do you stone me?" "We are not stoning you for any of these," replied the

101

Jews, **"but for blasphemy, because you, a mere man, claim to be God."** (John 10:31-33)

Many scholars use this verse to show us that Jesus claimed to be God. However consider Jesus' response:

Why then do you accuse me of blasphemy because I said, *'I am God's Son?'* Do not believe me unless I do what my Father does. But if I do it, even though you do not believe me, believe the miracles, that you may know and understand that the Father is in me, and I in the Father." (John 10:36-38 italics mine)

Jesus quotes Psalms 82:6, using the authority of Scripture to justify His position. What is His position? He said, "I am God's Son." Jesus did not claim to be God; *the Jews accused Him of such.* He pointed back to the Scriptures to show the graciousness of Yahweh to give the sons of men authority to become rulers who operate in His authority.

Jesus is Yahweh's Son

Many New Testament translations make the statement that Jesus and Yahweh are one in the same. This attempt is done by capitalizing the words 'I AM' and linking the God of the Old Testament to Jesus in a way that is not necessarily Biblical. 'I AM' is the phrase God gave Moses to tell the Israelites who He was. **God said to Moses, "I am who I am. This is what you are to say to the Israelites: I AM has sent me to you."** (Exodus 3:14)

In John 8:58, Jesus is simply stating the fact that He existed before Abraham. **"I tell you the truth," Jesus answered,**

"before Abraham was born, I am!" (John 8:58) Jesus used this phrase "I am" throughout the New Testament, as do other people, and without any special significance! I believe that many translators, when making the claim that Jesus was saying He was 'I AM', stretch the interpretation to fit their doctrinal preferences. As followers of Jesus, we must be aware of the unnecessary confusion this theology produces. If Jesus were saying that He was the 'I AM', most Jews would conclude that He was saying, "I am Yahweh Himself in the flesh." However, Jesus is not Yahweh; He is His Son!

Our message as Christians is that Jesus is restoring us back to God. Those under the Old Covenant were not able to be restored. Jesus had to come to mediate the covenant for you and I. May the church say to the Jew, like Ruth said to Naomi:

Don't urge me to leave you or to turn back from you. Where you go I will go, and where you stay I will stay. Your people will be my people and your God my God. (Ruth 1:16)

History shows us that Jesus has pointed millions of people throughout the world to worship the God of Israel. He has not brought them to 'other gods'. The way to the Father is now through the Son, to the Jew first, then to the rest of the world.

The Creeds were written in reaction to those who did not treat Jesus in the same way as they treated God Himself. The writers of the Creeds were zealous in their attempt to secure a High Christology, but did so, in my opinion, without fully relying on the Old Testament as a guide. A basic reading of the Bible points out that Jesus was not emphasized as God, so that He would not be confused with the Father. That title was mainly reserved for Yahweh. Jesus had no problem referring to

103

Himself as the 'Son of God'.

Simply the Son of God

Consider the following different sources from the New Testament concerning the person of Christ. The words 'divinity', 'Trinity' or 'Godhead', were never used in the sacred text; only Father and Son language. Every source declares Jesus is simply the Son of God.

1. How did Satan address Him?

The tempter came to him and said, "If you are the Son of God, tell these stones to become bread." (Matthew 4:3)

2. What did the demons say about Him?

"What do you want with us, Son of God?" they shouted. "Have you come here to torture us before the appointed time?" (Matthew 8:29)

3. What did His enemies say about Him?

He trusts in God. Let God rescue him now if he wants him, for he said, 'I am the Son of God.' (Matthew 27:43)

The Jews insisted, "We have a law, and according to that law he must die, because he claimed to be the Son of God." (John 19:7)

4. What did the Gentiles say about Him?

When the centurion and those with him who were guarding Jesus saw the earthquake and all that had happened, they were terrified, and exclaimed, "Surely he was the Son of God!" (Matthew 27:54)

5. How did the Gospels describe Him?

The beginning of the gospel about Jesus Christ, the Son of God... (Mark 1:1)

I have seen and I testify that this is the Son of God. (John 1:34) ·

But these are written that you may believe that Jesus is the Christ, the Son of God, and that by believing you may have life in his name. (John 20:31)

6. What did His disciples say about Him?

Then those who were in the boat worshiped him, saying, "Truly you are the Son of God." (Matthew 14:33)

7. What did the angels say about Him?

The angel answered, "The Holy Spirit will come upon you, and the power of the Most High will overshadow you. So the Holy one to be born will be called the Son of God." (Luke 1:35)

8. What did the Father say about Him?

And a voice came from heaven: "You are my Son, whom I love; with you I am well pleased." (Mark 1:11)

9. What did Jesus say about Himself?

They all asked, "Are you then the Son of God?" He replied, "You are right in saying I am." (Luke 22:7)

I am neither trying to attack nor justify the use of certain theological words. I have merely chosen to leave *that* language behind. I think the words Jesus left for us to define Him, and His relationship with His Father, are enough. I have heard some say that a Son is 'less' than the Father. That would make

105

Jesus a 'lesser' god. I would respond with the question, *"Why do we seek to understand God through a mathematical equation?"*

Jesus < Father

Jesus = Father

Father + Jesus + Spirit = 1

Maybe the deeper question remains, *"Is it right to use mathematical equations to describe the nature of God?"* The greatest statement that we need to rest on is that "God is love." He is not one, two or three. He is a God of love and a God of covenant. He is reaching out to this world; not just to our minds but to our hearts. He is a Father, longing to give birth to sons and daughters that He can call His own. Jesus is the true Son and we receive our adoption papers through His authority.

Dear friends, let us love one another, for love comes from God. Everyone who loves has been born of God and knows God. Whoever does not love does not know God, because God is love. This is how God showed his love among us: He sent his one and only Son into the world that we might live through him. (1 John 4:7-9)

A father is a picture all of us can relate to. Jesus taught his followers that the Father was a good Father.

If you then, though you are evil, know how to give good gifts to your children, how much more will your Father in heaven give the Holy Spirit to those who ask him! (Luke 11:13)

One day I was praying for my oldest son Michael and the

LORD asked me what I wanted most for him. I pondered the thought for a moment, and then said, *"I want him to feel alive!"* He then told me, *"I only desire the same for you!"* The Father empowers us inwardly by the Holy Spirit so that His power can flow outwardly to others. Good fathers give good gifts their children who ask.

A son reminds us of how we are to behave toward our Father. Jesus used the analogy of fathers and sons when referring to the kingdom.

What do you think? There was a man who had two sons. He went to the first and said, "Son, go and work today in the vineyard." "I will not," he answered, but later he changed his mind and went. Then the father went to the other son and said the same thing. He answered, "I will, sir," but he did not go. Which of the two did what his father wanted? "The first," they answered. (Matthew 21:28-32)

Our behavior flows out of our identity and our identity is connected to our perception of our Creator. God is far more concerned with 'who' we are instead of 'what' we do. We are called 'human beings' not 'human doings'. When we become authentic sons, we begin to behave like sons. Our identity is found in our son-ship and from this very identity we can complete our assignment. We should post signs in our gathering places, **"NO SONSHIP=NO SERVICE"**! In Jesus' very last moments, He does not ask John and Mary to 'do' something, He asks John and Mary to 'become' something. I believe that becoming not doing is the heart of the gospel message. Read Jesus' words to John:

When Jesus saw his mother there, and the disciple whom

107

he loved standing nearby, he said to his mother, "Dear woman, here is your son," and to the disciple, "Here is your mother." From that time on, this disciple took her into his home. (John 19:26-27)

The Heart of the Message

Theological language has often overlooked the most basic, simple and beautiful message; a Father empowering a Son to rule in His name, and a obedient Son fulfilling his Father's wishes. I earnestly pray that this message will become the core of our theology. What happens when the Father's message does not dominate? Researchers in Africa noted a strange occurrence in elephant herds when the dominant male of the herd was killed or removed. The young males of the herd would go rogue; rampaging in villages, acting wildly and distancing themselves from the other elephants. When the Father image is not present in the forefront of our theology, it will show up in our lives and in our gatherings. It is the presence of the Father that grounds us in who we are and how we behave. We have many out of control rogue Christians, because they have missed the strong presence of the Father God in their lives. The message of the Father God and His Son Jesus is imperative, causing us to hold our course, steady no matter what life brings. Electricity flows properly through a system of wires. One wire is the power wire and the other is the ground wire. Both must be connected to have useful power flowing. If you disconnect one wire, you will have no power. If you disconnect the other; the ground wire, you will have power, but you could be electrocuted!

Our doctrine forms a foundation and system of beliefs from which we live. Though I value praxology (what we practice) over theology, (doctrines we adhere to) I see that both are tied together. Teaching sound doctrine will contribute to good practices. Providing clarity in what we teach will cause us to value that which God values most. My paradigm tells me that God values relationship over 'rightness', and people over rules. From this perspective, we can reach the world in which we live with the love of the Father and give our lives for the gospel of Jesus Christ. The world needs to know Jesus because He is the way back to the Father.

Our understanding of Jesus and who He is, must be made clear. Jesus enables us to enter into covenant with the Father. Merely believing in God is not what 'saves' a person. Rather, it is believing in the Son of God, Jesus Christ, that brings salvation. I realize that this paradigm shift is a departure from mainstream theology. However, our theology should reflect the patterns of heaven and we must teach these patterns until they become the patterns of earth. The writer of Hebrews explains how this principle was applied to the tabernacle:

They serve at a sanctuary that is a copy and shadow of what is in heaven. This is why Moses was warned when he was about to build the tabernacle: "See to it that you make everything according to the pattern shown you on the mountain." (Hebrews 8:5)

I believe my calling is to simplify what man has complicated. I have had to work through my own fears of being labeled, losing face and being misunderstood. Will it be worth it? I believe it will. In the next chapter, we will look at the Scripture in the Old Testament used most often in the New Testament by Jesus and his followers that defined who He was. This Scripture is Psalm 110:1.

Reflection

1. Who do you say the Son of Man is?
2. Do you think Trinitarian language makes Christianity a hard sell to the Jew?
3. Though Trinitarian language fits into Greek thought and presents an orthodox view of Christ, does this model create confusion in how to approach God?
4. Is it right to use mathematical statements to describe the nature of God?
5. How would you respond to the question, "Is Jesus less than the Father?"

chapter eight
Lost in Translation

O ver the last decade, I have had the opportunity to take a few semesters of Greek and Hebrew during my seminary training. I do not relish the study of language as much as I enjoy theology. So in all of my language studies, my true desire was to better understand theology.

When we read the Bible, we sometimes forget that we are reading a translation. Some translations are better than others. Every translation will highlight and emphasize some points that others may ignore.

Haim Nachman Bialik, a Jewish Poet who lived from 1873-1934 said, *"Reading the Bible in translation is like kissing your new bride through a veil.'*[1] Since reading the writings in their original language is not possible for everyone, it is important to keep in mind how important the work of translation becomes.

The King James Version has a good example of a message lost in translation. The name 'James' is not found in the Bible! I discovered in the Greek text of the New Testament that the name 'James' is really the name 'Jacob'. The disciple 'James' is really the disciple 'Jacob' therefore the 'Book of James' is actually the 'Book of Jacob'. Some believe King James pressured the translators in 1611 to put his name in the Bible. All other English translations followed suit and so today most of us have never heard of Jesus' disciple named 'Jacob'!

It is important to study and compare translations while, at the same time, embracing what we are reading with confidence and trust. The Spirit of God will lead us as we study and we should read the Word as if we were fellowshipping with Jesus. Searching out the Scriptures in the original languages is a great way to uncover treasures hidden, waiting to be revealed.

One revelation I bumped into lately while studying Biblical Hebrew, was what it meant to be 'blessed' by God. Numbers 6:24 says, **"May the LORD bless you and keep you."** The Hebrew verb *barak* means to bless as seen in Genesis 12:2, but can also mean *kneel* as seen in Genesis 24:11. A related Hebrew word is *berakah* meaning a blessing, a gift, or present. From this we can see the concrete meaning behind *barak* in the sense of a blessing. It means, 'to bring a gift to another while kneeling out

---

[1] *Ancient Hebrew Research Center - Home Page.* Web. 16 Oct. 2010. <http://www.ancient-hebrew.org/>.

of respect.'[2]

With this understanding, we read the Aaronic blessing that is written in Numbers 6:24

Yahweh will kneel before you presenting gifts and will guard you with a hedge of protection, Yahweh will illuminate the wholeness of his being toward you bringing order and he will beautify you, Yahweh will lift up his wholeness of being and look upon you and he will set in place all you need to be whole and complete.[3]

To imagine the God of the universe kneeling before me melts me at the very core of who I am. I greatly desire the humility found in God Himself. When we take the time to study the words, we become enlightened with powerful revelation.

Most Quoted Verse

A few years ago I was reading over a Bible Quiz Book made for children and I came upon this question: What was the most quoted Old Testament scripture in the New Testament? Since then, I have been asking my Bible thumping friends if they knew the answer, and like me, they were stumped! I believe that as we study the ancient meaning of Psalm 110, the core of the gospel can be rediscovered. What is the message? Yahweh is elevating His Son to the highest place of honor- to sit at His right hand.

---

[2] Ibid.
[3] Ibid.

A powerful truth was hidden in the translation of Psalm 110:1 from the Hebrew and the Greek. (I do not believe this was done purposely...the error was made due to the understanding they had at the time.)   Like me, you have probably read these words of Jesus and His disciples without fully grasping their importance.

Jesus used Psalm 110 to convince His Jewish brethren of who He was. Other New Testament authors often allude to its content as well, when pointing to who Jesus actually is. **"The LORD says to my Lord: 'Sit at my right hand until I make your enemies a footstool for your feet.'"** (Psalm 110:1)

When we translate the most important scripture in the Old Testament that best explains the role of the Messiah, we say **"The LORD said to my Lord..."** This sounds a bit confusing, and is so vague that we are left to draw conclusions that can lead us astray.

As we discussed in the fourth chapter, God has one name; Yahweh. Yahweh assumes the title of "God" and this is the name of our Heavenly Father. The name is four letters in Hebrew, YHVH, which most Jews refuse to say because His Name is considered sacred. Most often, the name 'Yahweh' was translated as LORD. (All Capital Letters)

In the New Testament we find Jesus assuming the title of Lord. This title is a key in understanding Psalm 110:1. The word in Hebrew for Lord (*not* all capitalized letters) is *Adonai* or *Adon*. This is the actual word in Hebrew for Lord and points most often to the person of Jesus.

Translating Psalm 110:1 from the perspective of a first

Century Jew, it would most likely be understood as, "Yahweh (The LORD) says to Jesus, (my Lord) sit at my right hand until I (Yahweh) make our enemies a footstool for your feet."

Our Jewish brethren felt it was honoring to keep the name of Yahweh sacred by not saying His name. Instead, Jews would use the word LORD when referring to the personal name of God. Because of this translation issue, Psalm 110:1 has not been understood and its impact has been neutralized.

Psalm 110 and the book of Hebrews

I recently did a study on the book of Hebrews. I had not realized that the first 12 chapters of the book of Hebrews are an explanation of Psalm 110. Psalm 110 was the very resource early Jews used to prove Jesus was the Messiah. Yet, most Christians, like myself, had no clue about the importance of these seven verses.

Many scholars believe the book of Hebrews was written to the priests who were serving in the Temple in Jerusalem. They seemed to be confused about the purpose and identity of Jesus Christ.

I believe the author of Hebrews may have been Luke, the doctor, who also wrote the gospel of Luke and the book of Acts. As we begin to study Hebrews, I will show you the strong connection between this book and Psalm 110.

In the past God spoke to our forefathers through the prophets at many times and in various ways, but in these last days he has spoken to us by his Son, whom he appointed heir of all things, and through whom he made

the universe. (Hebrews 1:1-2)

Jesus Christ is the heir of the kingdom of God and He is the final Word. As a Jew, this must have been a radical thought. Jesus was not pointing the Jews to another God, but to His Son as the door to salvation for all mankind.

The Son is the radiance of God's glory and the exact representation of his being, sustaining all things by his powerful word. After he had provided purification for sins, he sat down at the right hand of the Majesty in heaven... (Hebrew 1:3)

To the recipients of the letter of Hebrews, the author was clarifying that Jesus was also much more than an angel. Very likely, many Jews struggled with the concept of God having a Son. For this the writer of Hebrews asked the question:

For to which of the angels did God ever say, "You are my Son; today I have become your Father." Or again, "I will be his Father, and he will be my Son"? (Hebrews 1:5)

Most scholars overlook the importance of Psalm 110 and few realize the book of Hebrews uses it for the 'proof text' of how we ought to view Jesus. The throne of Yahweh, His power and kingdom are being fulfilled through His Son. Yahweh's dynasty is fulfilled through the ascension of Jesus Christ.

The Ascension of Christ

Very little emphasis is placed upon the ascension of Christ to the throne. Maybe we are hesitant because the question may arise; "Wasn't Christ always on the throne?" My view is that Christ ascended to the throne after His resurrection for the purpose of ruling here on earth. I believe that He had always ruled with the Father prior to His ascension, but now is taking the prominent role in bringing restoration to the earth. When we talk about the Father and Son being one, it is in reference to the throne on which they sit.

But about the Son he says, "Your throne, O God, will last forever and ever, and righteousness will be the scepter of your kingdom. You have loved righteousness and hated wickedness; therefore God, your God, has set you above your companions by anointing you with the oil of joy." (Hebrews 1:8-9)

All believers have access to the Father through the Son. God's throne will rule over the earth through the church because of who is now seated at His right hand. Jesus is not an angel; He is the Risen Son of God.

Every king sought to have his kingdom continue on after his death through a faithful son. Yet there is little emphasis on the ascension of Christ to the throne in modern theology. The emphasis can be clearly seen in the following scriptures in the New Testament.

"Yes, it is as you say," Jesus replied. "But I say to all of you: In the future you will see the Son of Man sitting at the right hand of the Mighty One and coming on the clouds of heaven." (Matthew 26:64)

"I am," said Jesus. "And you will see the Son of Man sitting at the right hand of the Mighty One and coming on the clouds of heaven." (Mark 14:62)

After the Lord Jesus had spoken to them, he was taken up into heaven and he sat at the right hand of God. (Mark 16:19)

But from now on, the Son of Man will be seated at the right hand of the mighty God. (Luke 22:69)

But Stephen, full of the Holy Spirit, looked up to heaven and saw the glory of God, and Jesus standing at the right hand of God. (Acts 7:55)

"Look," he said, "I see heaven open and the Son of Man standing at the right hand of God." (Acts 7:56)

Who is he that condemns? Christ Jesus, who died—more than that, who was raised to life—is at the right hand of God and is also interceding for us. (Romans 8:34)

Since, then, you have been raised with Christ, set your hearts on things above, where Christ is seated at the right hand of God. (Colossians 3:1)

Meditating on these Scriptures has given me new insight into many of my own unanswered questions in the Bible. For example, I had always wondered why Jesus must return and then Satan is released again after one thousand years. In light of the rule of the Son, we find Jesus returning, setting up His kingdom on earth and reigning for a Millennium. (1,000 year reign) At the end of His reign, Satan will be released so that the Son can put him under His feet once and for all. At this point, the New Jerusalem will come down from heaven and the earth will be fully restored.

Then the end will come, when He hands over the kingdom to God the Father after he has destroyed all dominion, authority and power. For he must reign until He has put all His enemies under his feet. The last enemy to be destroyed is death. For he, 'has put everything under his feet.' Now when it says that 'everything' has been put under him, it is clear that this does not include God himself, who put everything under Christ. When he has done this, then the Son himself will be made subject to him who put everything under him, so that God may be all in all. (1 Corinthians 15:24-28)

What a beautiful picture we have of the Father releasing His complete authority to His Son! How great a God we serve who is unafraid to let another rule in His Name! He is a Father who wants to raise sons and daughters that look and act just like Him. Jesus is our model as the perfect son, making the way for us to follow Him into our sonship by the Holy Spirit.

For you did not receive a spirit that makes you a slave again to fear, but you received the Spirit of sonship. And by him we cry, 'Abba, Father.' (Romans 8:15)

The Spirit of God is the confirmation of our heavenly adoption papers that were purchased through the death of Jesus. We are now connected to the Father in the name of Jesus through Spirit.

Because you are sons, God sent the Spirit of his Son into our hearts, the Spirit who calls out, 'Abba, Father.' (Galatians 4:6)

The Psalm describes the raising up of a Son to rule the earth. Jesus is the successor to the throne of His Father. The psalmist writes:

The LORD will extend your mighty scepter from Zion, saying, 'Rule in the midst of your enemies! Your troops will be willing on your day of battle. Arrayed in holy splendor, your young men will come to you like dew from the morning's womb. The LORD has sworn and will not change his mind: "You are a priest forever, in the order of Melchizedek." The Lord is at your right hand; he will crush kings on the day of his wrath. He will judge the nations, heaping up the dead and crushing the rulers of the whole earth. (Psalm 110:2-7)

The LORD is Yahweh and *the Lord* is Jesus. This verse reminds us that Jesus will rule the world in righteousness and establish His government on earth. The Father has extended His dynasty through His Son. In the next chapter we will consider the stumbling blocks that cause people to stumble and fall.

Reflection

1. Almost all translations of Psalm 110 use the words LORD and Lord. What is the meaning behind these words?
2. There are hundreds of different translations of the Bible available for us. How should you chose which Bible translation to use?
3. Why do you think Psalm 110:1 was the most quoted Old Testament verse in the New Testament?
4. We hear that Jesus rose from the dead, but rarely that He also ascended to the right hand. Is the ascension of Jesus to the throne of the Father overlooked in modern theology?

chapter nine
Stumbling Blocks

*I*n our understanding of God, we must begin with a Biblical understanding that is rooted in the Old Testament and worked out through the New Testament. The Old Testament is the New Testament concealed. The New Testament is the Old Testament revealed.

Jesus came to the Jewish people being born a Jew. Initially he even rejected ministering to Gentiles saying, **"I was sent only to the lost sheep of Israel."** (Matthew 15:24) Remember that all of Jesus' followers were Jewish and the entire New Testament was written by Jews, except for Luke, Acts and possibly the book of Hebrews. Jesus revealed Himself to the Jews and expected them to take the gospel, from their perspective, to the world.

Established in Jewish culture is an ingrained understanding of generational blessing. The idea of Heaven's dynasty flowing through a Son is a pattern already established in ceremonies and traditions familiar to our Jewish counterpart. I believe the lack of emphasis on God as Father and Jesus as Son has hindered the gospel message among the Jews. I believe Jesus is to be the only stumbling block. In this chapter, we will examine how the 'Three in One' view of God may be an unnecessary cause of stumbling.

In this chapter, I also want to present a perspective from the Old Testament of who the Jews were expecting the Messiah to be. The Jews as a people group have rejected Jesus as the Messiah. In turn, much of our own Christian theology is lacking. The formation of the Trinitarian model may have been a result of this void. From there, we can see how Jesus came as the Son of Yahweh, the Son of God; The Messiah.

As I teach about the Jewish rejection of Jesus, many ask, "How could they miss the obvious?" In one sense, there is a spiritual blindness over their eyes. Paul writes about this in his letter to the Corinthians:

But their minds were made dull, for to this day the same veil remains when the old covenant is read. It has not been removed, because only in Christ is it taken away. Even to this day when Moses is read, a veil covers their hearts. But whenever anyone turns to the Lord, the veil is taken away. (2 Corinthians 3:14-16)

I used to go to a college campus on a weekly basis to share

my faith with the students. I had a friend who would accompany me as we shared the good news. One day while we were witnessing to a person, my friend began explaining the Trinity to an unsaved person. After this unfruitful discussion, I asked him if he felt it was necessary to bring up the Trinity. From that day forward I began to realize how illogical this doctrine might appear to an outsider. I was reminded that we must not create any stumbling blocks that would keep people from receiving Jesus as Lord.

God has pointed to the rock that will make man stumble-His Son Jesus Christ. When a Jew stumbles, it may be because they lack the full understanding of the message. As Christians, we have a responsibility to clearly explain what we believe in order to bring understanding. Listen to the parable of the sower:

When anyone hears the message about the kingdom and does not *understand* it, the evil one comes and snatches away what was sown in his heart... (Matthew 13:19 italics mine)

We take authority away from the evil one when we explain the message in a clear manner. Lord, help us clearly present who You are, in light of what You have already said- especially to the lost sheep of Israel!

A Prophet Like Moses

In Deuteronomy 18, the LORD spoke to Moses concerning this coming Son. Moses actually prophesies about a coming Prophet that would be very much like Moses himself. The Prophet and the Messiah were not understood as one in the same, but clearly Jesus fulfilled both. Consider the following scripture in which the LORD is speaking to Moses:

I will raise up for them a prophet like you from among their brothers; I will put my words in his mouth and he will tell them everything I command him. If anyone does not listen to my words that the prophet speaks in my name, I myself will call him to account. (Deut. 18:18-19)

This coming prophet will be like Moses. Throughout the passage, the singular use of the word prophet is used. No other prophet from among the Israelites has risen to compare with Jesus.

Moses worked great miracles, which had important national impact. Elijah and Elisha were other miracle workers, but acted more in private than in public. In comparison to the power in which Moses worked miracles, only Jesus can compare to the miracle ministry of Moses. After the feeding of the five thousand, the people said of Jesus, **"Surely this is the Prophet who is to come into the world."** (John 6:14)

Moses was a lawgiver, covenant maker and teacher. His teachings carried great authority unlike any other Old Testament prophet. As Moses brought a people into covenant with God, so Jesus brought a people into covenant with God through His own blood. (Luke 22:20) No other teacher has had such profound influence upon Jewish thought since the time of Moses.

Moses was a deliverer and mediator. What other prophet delivered masses of people from bondage, (Exodus 13) and stood between God and the people as a mediator, fasting forty days and forty nights? (Deuteronomy 9:18) What other Jewish figure ever offered up his life, as in Deuteronomy 32:32, **"But now, please forgive their sin- but if not, then blot me out of the book you have written"...**, for the sin of a rebellious people? May all of Israel say, like the Jews who heard Jesus at the feast of Tabernacles: **"Surely this man is the Prophet."** (John 7:40)

Do-It-Yourself Salvation

At the time Jesus came to earth, the Jews were devout in following the Law of Moses. But instead of drawing them closer to God, it became a system of doing, without any real need for relationship. As a remedy, God gave them a place of rest from works righteousness in the person of Jesus. However, most of the Jews refused to enter into that rest God had provided for them.

I see this mentality very often in ministry. I call it "Do-It-Yourself" salvation. We create an atmosphere of *performance-based acceptance* when we emphasize rules over relationship. Performance driven people continually try to follow the rules so that they can experience the acceptance of their Heavenly Father, instead of resting in the acceptance that is found in Jesus' blood sacrifice. As the hymn says, "This is all my righteousness, nothing but the blood of Jesus. Not for good that I have done, nothing but the blood of Jesus."[1]

Isaiah speaks of a time when Gentiles will proclaim a resting

---

[1] *CCLI: Global.* Web. 2 Nov. 2010. <http://www.ccli.com/>.

place for the Jewish people. But because the Jew would not listen, the word of the LORD to them has not resulted in freedom.

With foreign lips and strange tongues God will speak to this people, to whom he said, "This is the resting place, let the weary rest," and, "This is the place of repose"--but they would not listen. So then, the word of the LORD to them will become: Do and do, do and do, rule on rule, rule on rule; a little here, a little there--so that they will go and fall backward, be injured and snared and captured. (Isaiah 28:11-13)

Salvation could never be accomplished through 'doing'. When a person does not feel the pleasure of God upon his or her life, the end result will be a pursuit of doing good works, participating in religious activities. World religions have created complicated systems of works in hopes of appeasing God. When a person accomplishes this system of works created to appease their Creator, the result will not be humility or dependence on God. The apostle Paul writes that salvation is a gift received by faith, not acquired through works.

For it is by grace you have been saved, through faith—and this not from yourselves, it is the gift of God— not by works, so that no one can boast. (Ephesians 2:8-9)

To the religious, works driven God seeker, the above statement is a scandal! They are proud of their own accomplishments to appease God and then someone comes along and declares that salvation is a gift! Paul describes this exact situation in his letter to the Christians in Rome.

What then shall we say? That the Gentiles, who did not

pursue righteousness, have obtained it, a righteousness that is by faith; but Israel, who pursued a law of righteousness, has not attained it. Why not? Because they pursued it not by faith, but as if it were by works. They stumbled over the 'stumbling stone.' As it is written: "See, I lay in Zion a stone that causes men to stumble and a rock that makes them fall, and the one who trusts in him will never be put to shame." (Romans 9:30-33)

Sadly, the Jews would stumble upon the rock- the rock Jesus Christ. He is the cornerstone referred to in the book of Isaiah. He is the cause of the stumbling because righteousness is attained through Him alone. This was a very difficult message for 1st Century Jews.

For in the gospel a righteousness from God is revealed, a righteousness that is by faith from first to last, just as it is written: "The righteous will live by faith." (Romans 1:17)

We also read In Isaiah 28 that foreign lips and strange tongues will speak to the house of Israel. Can you see how God is preparing the Jews to hear from foreigners that righteousness is for those who believe and not by works?

Fully Receiving All His Love

Righteousness, or right standing with God, comes only to those who receive it freely. Many Christians have not experienced this revelation fully. Many of us do not feel 'good' enough to receive the free gift of salvation. A trap is released upon our life when this feeling of unworthiness is not addressed. We engage in church attendance, programs and missions giving, only to suffer burnout in the short run, because adding our works to what Jesus has done, actually nullifies His work!

My own experience in life is that of a emotionally hurt young man. I was raised in a nominal Catholic home only later to have an encounter with Jesus in my dorm room while at Penn State University. This encounter led me to open my heart to receiving the sacrifice of Jesus for my sins a few months later.

Throughout most of my Christian life though, I had a difficult time receiving love. I could give love and do good things for people, but I had to be on the giving end. I was very prideful, yet I cloaked it in false humility. Establishing myself on the giving end of things is probably what motivated me to enter into ministry!

The reality is that if you cannot freely receive love, then you cannot freely give it! A gift then has strings attached! Whenever someone gave me something freely, the giver meant to convey a message that said, "You have value and worth because of who you are!" Yet my heart felt the need to repay them because of my distorted view of love. I felt worthless on the inside and this feeling was exposed whenever I was given something freely.

I can remember my first mission's trip to Daytona Beach with Campus Crusade for Christ. We spent our spring break sharing the gospel and winning souls on the beaches where thousands of college students had gone to party. I led many people to Christ that week and had been empowered in the Spirit for the first time in my life. I felt a power and freedom like never before.

On the bus ride home, a young man purchased a $6.00 t-shirt and gave it to me as a gift. I had run out of money and he decided to get one for me. Something happened inside of me that caused me to avoid this young man from that point forward. I could not tell you 'why' I felt that way toward him then, but I think now I understand the 'why.' I had to avoid him because I did not feel worthy to receive anything freely at that point in my life. His action made me feel obligated to repay him because I felt unworthy to receive. His actions exposed the lie I believed about myself.

You are never too poor to give and never too rich to receive. Everything we have is because we have received from our Father above first. I tell people, "I am like a blind squirrel that bumped into an acorn!" The joy in what I have discovered and now freely receive, is my main motivation in bringing heaven to earth!

Presenting Jesus to the Jews

Many of the Jews in the time of Jesus had attained a system of righteousness that was very difficult to achieve. Jesus came to expose the pride of works driven salvation. I believe that Israel as a nation stumbled in the 1st Century and missed the Messiah because of the pride of self-righteousness. But they have not stumbled beyond recovery.

I say then, "Have they stumbled that they should fall? God forbid: but rather through their fall salvation is come unto the Gentiles, for to provoke them to jealousy." (Romans 11:11 King James Version)

Historically, the church has provoked Israel, but not to

131

jealousy.   Saint Augustine, one of the most influential theologians in our Christian heritage, said of the Jews in his day, "Let them live among us, but let them suffer and be continually humiliated."[2]   Augustine planted a seed of Anti-Semitism that would later produce a harvest of Jewish bloodshed.

The Jews missed their Messiah, but we must not place any other stumbling blocks in their way.   Christian Anti-Semitism, the Crusades, and our complicated theology have provoked the Jews, but not to jealousy.

Since they did not know the righteousness that comes from God and sought to establish their own, they did not submit to God's righteousness. Christ is the end of the law so that there may be righteousness for everyone who believes. (Romans 10:3-4)

When Christ referred to "the end of the law," the Greek word for 'end' is *telios*. It means, "to set out for a definite point or goal; properly, the point aimed at as a limit, the conclusion of an act or state." [3] Everything Christ stood for completed the purpose of the Mosaic Laws.

Isaiah 28 alludes to the people of Israel **"...will go and fall backward, be injured and snared and captured."** A snare is something metaphorically that lures one from his real purpose

---

[2] "The Guilt of Christianity Towards the Jewish People - Anti-Semitism and Holocaust." *Christian Action for Israel.* Web. 18 Dec. 2010.
[3] Zodhiates, Spiros, and John R. Kohlenberger. *The Hebrew-Greek Key Study Bible: New International Version.* Chattanooga, TN: AMG Pub., 1996. 1679.

and then destroys him.[4]   When we think we can attain righteousness through our own works, it becomes a snare to us! But just like it happened to many Jews in the time of Jesus, beware that it does not happen to you!   We must not let the word of the Lord become "do and do and rule on rule" and refuse to enter His rest. Jesus literally became the Sabbath rest for His people.   *Our work is not for salvation but from salvation.*   We must end our striving for righteousness, and learn to simply and fully receive it.

The Rejected Capstone

Jesus used the picture in describing Himself as the capstone that the builders rejected. He gave only two choices in regards to this stone- fall upon it, or it will fall on you!

Jesus looked directly at them and asked, "Then what is the meaning of that which is written: 'The stone the builders rejected has become the capstone?'   Everyone who falls on that stone will be broken to pieces, but he on whom it falls will be crushed." (Luke 20:17-18)

I like the picture of falling on Jesus. It is that place of total surrender in what Jesus has done for me. I fall into His arms and His mercy and I am safe: no more striving for righteousness or even trying to add to what He has done. When Jesus died on the cross he said, **"It is finished."** He is the One who makes us righteous through His blood.   The only

---

[4] Harris, R. Laird, Gleason L. Archer, and Bruce K. Waltke. *Theological Wordbook of the Old Testament.* Chicago: Moody, 1980. 399. Print.

133

stumbling block that should remain is the person of Jesus Christ.

As it is written: "See, I lay in Zion a stone that causes men to stumble and a rock that makes them fall, and the one who trusts in him will never be put to shame." (Romans 9:33)

Listen To The Son

When we minister to Jews and Muslims, we find that many of them have a heart for the Creator, and are attempting to worship Him. Though seeking God is commendable, we must give them the complete message: you must acknowledge the Son Jesus Christ as Lord. The Father has commanded men of the earth to obey the voice of Jesus: **"A voice came from the cloud, saying, 'This is my Son, whom I have chosen; listen to him.'"** (Luke 9:35)

As we look at mankind reaching out to their Creator, the picture becomes very clear. Because they could not fathom His love or His holiness, they developed rules and ceremonies to try and appease the Creator. Since they were unable to experience the power and love of their Creator, they turned to other sources.

As we reach out into our world, we acknowledge that seeking to please the Creator is noble, but the answer is not found in ceremonies or sacrifices. The only way to please the Creator is to honor and acknowledge His Son. Jesus is the accepted way the Father has provided to come back to Him. Rejecting Jesus means you also reject the kingdom of God. We cannot please the Creator any other way. God has given us the very best He could give; His One and Only Son.

Jesus is the Middle Man

In our Christian witness, I believe our message will lack clarity if we claim that *Jesus is God*, instead of emphasizing He is *God's Son*. We know that the only saving source in the universe is the blood of Jesus Christ. He is the mediator *between* man and God.

For there is one God and one mediator between God and men, the man Christ Jesus, who gave himself as a ransom for all men." (1 Timothy 2:5-6)

Many people are hesitant to talk about the man Christ Jesus. However, being a man is not an insult! Jesus Himself became a man so that we could relate to the Father, not from a distance, but as a son or daughter.

In business, we always want to eliminate the middleman. The middleman drives up expenses so that we want to go directly to the source. In America there is a huge debate over the cost of medical insurance. Insurance is supposed to be a mediator between our source of health and us. But the cost of medical insurance alone can make us sick!

Yet on the other hand, a mediator in some situations is the only way a conflict can be resolved. Many people today are trying to eliminate the middleman out of their spiritual life. They want to go directly to God. The problem is that going directly to God without Jesus Christ is a sure way to die! Jesus fulfilled the terms of the covenant that God demanded. A good

135

mediator was the only solution. The word covenant can also be translated as testament, from which we get the 'New Testament' or 'New Covenant' which declares to us:

For this reason Christ is the mediator of a new covenant, that those who are called may receive the promised eternal inheritance, now that he has died as a ransom to set them free from the sins committed under the first covenant. (Hebrews 9:15)

The requirement of our ransom could only be paid by the blood of a sinless man. This requirement was fulfilled in Jesus, as the author of Hebrews tells us:

You have come to God, the judge of all men, to the spirits of righteous men made perfect, to Jesus the mediator of a new covenant, and to the sprinkled blood that speaks a better word than the blood of Abel. (Hebrews 12:23-24)

As Christians, we must emphasize the power of Jesus to forgive man of sin and bring them into covenant with God. Jesus is the answer Job was crying out for in the midst of his trial:

Yet if there is an angel on his side as a mediator, one out of a thousand, to tell a man what is right for him, to be gracious to him and say, 'Spare him from going down to the pit; I have found a ransom for him'- then his flesh is renewed like a child's; it is restored as in the days of his youth. He prays to God and finds favor with him, he sees God's face and shouts for joy; he is restored by God to his righteous state. Then he comes to men and says, 'I sinned, and perverted what was right, but I did not get

what I deserved. He redeemed my soul from going down to the pit, and I will live to enjoy the light.' (Job 33:23-28)

Jesus is the middleman, the *mesos* in the Greek, meaning "the go between, the middle."[5] In this role, Jesus becomes the priest, the one who stands in the place of intercession for us. **"Christ Jesus, who died, more than that, who was raised to life, is at the right hand of God and is also interceding for us."** (Romans 8:34)

I love the picture of Jesus interceding for us. The world always tells us- "When you're in trouble, be sure you have a good lawyer!" Thankfully, we have one great defense lawyer, who understands our weaknesses, yet has overcome the world and won our righteousness! Jesus identifies with the Spirit as an intercessor, and this intercessor lives in us!

In the same way, the Spirit helps us in our weakness. We do not know what we ought to pray for, but the Spirit himself intercedes for us with groans that words cannot express. And he who searches our hearts knows the mind of the Spirit, because the Spirit intercedes for the saints in accordance with God's will. (Romans 8:26-27)

---

[5] Zodhiates, Spiros, and John R. Kohlenberger. *The Hebrew-Greek Key Study Bible: New International Version*. Chattanooga, TN: AMG Pub., 1996. 1650.

137

Reflection

1. Have you ever had trouble explaining the Trinity? Would you consider the Trinity a possible stumbling block to the message of understanding who Jesus is?

2. The Jews were told that God would raise up a prophet like Moses and were commanded to listen to him. Describe how Jesus was like Moses more than any other prophet in Israel's history.

3. Describe how Jesus was **"the rock that caused man to stumble."** How did the concept of righteousness by faith versus performance-based righteousness cause many to fall?

4. Jesus said, **"Everyone who falls on that stone will be broken to pieces, but he on whom it falls will be crushed."** (Luke 20:18) How does the picture of "falling on Jesus" relate to how we are saved?

5. The Bible teaches we must point the world to Jesus, God's Son, for salvation. How have many people become trapped in trying to 'do' salvation instead of 'being' saved?

6. Have you ever been given a gift that felt unworthy to receive it? The next time someone gives you something or does something for you, just say "Thank you" and receive it freely. You are worth the blood of God's Son and you were bought at a great price!

7. Jesus is the mediator of the New Covenant or the middleman between God and us. Do you think the world wants to bypass the Son and go directly to the Father? What are the results that many religious people face when attempting to bypass the middleman?

chapter ten
What about the
Holy Spirit?

Many ask at this point, "What about the Holy Spirit?" This is a logical question and one I must to address. I have been wrestling Scripture hoping to make the gospel clearly understandable to everyday people in reference to the Spirit of God.

As I was writing this manuscript, I must share with you a funny story. For some strange reason, I had always read in Mathew 3:16 that the Holy Spirit descended on Jesus like a dove and *lightning* upon Him. I can remember teaching how the Holy Spirit is gentle like a dove and powerful like lightning! This preached well, but was totally misread. I even contacted an online Bible source to correct them on their mistranslation because I was so convinced! They assured me that they had the right translation that, **"The Holy Spirit descended like a dove and *lighted* upon Him!"** (Matthew 3:16).

After realizing my theological blunder, I realized how easy it is to miss the obvious. Though I wanted to crawl under my chair, I decided to laugh at myself. God has a sense of humor. I am sure that I now have your utmost confidence in my ability to translate the Bible- especially concerning the Holy Spirit!

I think this will be a helpful study of the Word of God that will present a wider view of the work of the Spirit. These thoughts may be challenging to some, but may bring clarity to some of the statements found in Scripture. Truth is discovered and empowered by the Spirit.

The Breath of God

The Greek word for spirit is *pneuma* and the word in Hebrew is *ruach*. Both words mean "spirit, breath or wind." Consider this thought in light of Genesis 2:7:

The LORD God formed the man from the dust of the ground and breathed into his nostrils the breath of life, and the man became a living being. (Genesis 2:7)

In the most basic understanding of the word *spirit*, "breath" is the main emphasis; breath that brings life. Breath is the distinction between what is alive and what is dead. When someone says, "The meeting was dead," they are saying the meeting lacked the life of the Spirit.

140

Breath originates from someone! The Spirit is the life that flows from the Father and the Son to those who need resuscitation! The breath of God is the atmosphere of heaven, which *does not* have earthly origin. God breathed into Adam and he became a living being. God poured out His Spirit upon the church in Acts chapter two and the body of Christ here on earth came alive!

When the day of Pentecost came, they were all together in one place. Suddenly a sound like the blowing of a violent wind came from heaven and filled the whole house where they were sitting. They saw what seemed to be tongues of fire that separated and came to rest on each of them. All of them were filled with the Holy Spirit and began to speak in other tongues as the Spirit enabled them. (Acts 2:1-4)

The Kingdom of God

The Spirit is poured out as the kingdom of God is released on earth. We rarely consider the correlation between Jesus' ascension to the throne and the release of the Holy Spirit upon the body of Christ on earth. The Holy Spirit and the Kingdom of God flow together. The reason the Holy Spirit could be poured out upon **"everyone who called upon the name of the Lord"** is because Jesus became the temple of the Holy Spirit on earth. **"Don't you know that you yourselves are God's temple and that God's Spirit lives in you?"** (1 Corinthians 3:16)

As the Holy Spirit fills the temple of the human body, the Spirit also fills the body of Christ. The church is the *ecclesia* or "the called out ones." As we gather in the name of Jesus, we have the promise of His presence that we can experience together.

141

In the last days, God says, "I will pour out my Spirit on all people. Your sons and daughters will prophesy, your young men will see visions, your old men will dream dreams. Even on my servants, both men and women, I will pour out my Spirit in those days, and they will prophesy." (Acts 2:17-18)

The Spirit is to believers, what good wireless Internet access is to computer users. With good Internet access, you have access to information, tools, relationships and connections that would otherwise be impossible. The world is at your fingertips.

In the modern world, we are always searching for ways to acquire better, faster and more reliable Internet service. There is a need for an Internet provider to install a system that will allow you access to the World Wide Web. The more you are willing to pay each month determines the level of access you will receive.

When the church entered into the 20th century, the Holy Spirit became a renewed focus for many Christians. Pope Leo XIII renewed the focus on the Holy Spirit in his January 1, 1901 message to the world. On that same day, a Bible school in Topeka, Kansas experienced the gifts of the Spirit, including speaking in tongues.[1] Something shifted on that day.

I believe the church was wired in that day to the kingdom of God with renewed access. The gifts of the Spirit represent the

---

[1] History of the Catholic Charismatic Renewal." *Arlington Diocese - Catholic Charismatic Renewal*. Web. 23 Mar. 2011. <http://www.arlingtonrenewal.org/history>.

tools or apps every Christian needs to advance the kingdom of God. The Holy Spirit is the Internet connection the church needs to fulfill the our destiny of restoring the planet.

As the church was wired in at the beginning of the 20th century, I believe the 21st century is calling us to go 'wireless'. I recently purchased a phone that has a feature called a 'mobile hotspot'. Wherever I go, I have access to the World Wide Web, without wires and with complete mobility.

The work of the Spirit has often been limited to four walls of the building where the church gathers. In my opinion, the true test is to see the kingdom of God released in its fullness inside *and* outside. Each us of have a mobile hotspot to which we can offer the world access to the kingdom of God.

We must engage in kingdom activity to activate the kingdom here on earth. The reason we worship, pray and preach is because these actions stir up the Spirit in us, and in our gathering times. The Spirit moves upon us so that healings come, revelation comes, restoration comes and we encounter Jesus. He said to his followers that **"…the kingdom of heaven has been forcefully advancing, and forceful men lay hold of it."** (Matthew 11:12)

Advancing the kingdom of God requires us to confront the kingdom of darkness. Throughout the gospels, we read about unclean spirits that came upon people. Jesus simply spoke the word and they were delivered. The contrast to what is unclean is that which is holy. The Kingdom of God is advancing as unclean spirits are being cast out. Jesus said, **"But if I drive out demons by the finger of God, then the kingdom of God has come to you!"** (Luke 11:20)

143

Have you ever wondered why the emphasis of the Spirit is on holiness instead of faith, hope or love? *Our actions will determine the spirit that is working in us.* How can we stand for righteousness if our actions are unrighteous? The prophet Micah declared, **"But as for me, I am filled with power, with the Spirit of the LORD, and with justice and might, to declare to Jacob his transgression, to Israel his sin."** (Micah 3:8)

Evil spirits in the New Testament are actually called 'unclean spirits'. When people do evil things and have evil thoughts, they become unclean and attract the spirit of uncleanness. The opposite holds true for those who pursue righteousness: they become inhabited by the spirit of holiness (i.e. the Holy Spirit). Demonic possession needs to be encountered with Holy Spirit possession.

I Thought You Were a Ghost?

In reference to the Holy Spirit, the King James Version translates the word *spirit* as "ghost." This version of the Bible has had a tremendous influence on theology and has promoted a 'Holy Ghost' instead of a Spirit. The King James translation implies a separate personality instead of the breath of Someone.

The word for 'ghost' in the Greek language is *phantom*. The word in the Greek language for 'spirit' is *pneuma*. *Pneuma* is always linked in meaning to 'breath' or 'wind'.

When the word 'ghost' is used in Scripture, it brings fear! **"When the disciples saw him walking on the lake, they were terrified. 'It's a ghost,' they said, and cried out in fear."** (Matthew 14:26) Perhaps it would be prudent to hesitate in referring to the Holy Spirit as the Holy Ghost, because words carry meaning. We must think carefully how to best communicate the truth of the Scriptures to the world.

I believe the early disciples were empowered by the Spirit and after Pentecost were able to walk with the Lord again. This view seems to bring better continuity to the Scriptures than viewing the Holy Spirit as a separate distinct person. Paul declares, **"I have been crucified with Christ and I no longer live, but Christ lives in me."**(Galatians 2:20) Christ lives inside of us via our Spirit connection and through our acknowledgement of who Jesus is, we have our fullness in God. Jesus is our access code and there is no other name that connects us to the kingdom! John writes, **"If anyone acknowledges that Jesus is the Son of God, God lives in him and he in God."** (1 John 4:15)

In our local Bible School training, one of my students came to me with this analogy. A cell phone receives a signal from a tower that rises up from the earth. As the phone connects to the tower, the signal is broadcast to a satellite located in the heavens. As long as all three parts of this equation are working, the phone, the tower and the satellite, a connection occurs.

In this analogy, the phone represents my Spirit connection. The tower represents the victory purchased for me at the cross by Jesus Christ. The satellite represents my heavenly Father who communicates to me from above. The higher the tower, the better the connection there will be in the area surrounding the tower. I am reminded what Jesus said, **"But I, when I am lifted up from the earth, will draw all men to myself."** (John 12:32)

Establishing the kingdom of God on earth is all about lifting up Jesus! As we lift up Jesus, the world will be connected into the kingdom of God. The Kingdom *realized* is the Kingdom *released*! Jesus told His disciples that **"It is for your good that I am going away."** (John 16:7) When Jesus was seated at the right hand of the Father, He then released His authority to us and give us His breath and His life. After Jesus' resurrection, Jesus spoke to His disciples and also released life into them. How did He do this? **"And with that he breathed on them and said, 'Receive the Holy Spirit.'"**(John 20:22)

Jesus said in John 6:63, **"The Spirit gives life."** I have an image of Jesus taking a deep breath and then exhaling, filling His church with the Spirit of God. Breathing is actually a picture of rest and relaxation. We are not working for our salvation, but simply receiving our eternal life as we trust in Jesus Christ.

The Spirit: Earth, Wind and Fire

The Spirit is like a fire, burning in our hearts, that we must *keep* burning. Paul commands believers, **"Do not put out the Spirit's fire."** (1Thessalonians 5:19) John the Baptist said concerning Jesus, **"...after me will come one who is more powerful than I... He will baptize you with the Holy Spirit and with fire."** (Matthew 3:11)

I have a rather large backyard that keeps our family busy collecting sticks and leaves. We usually have a pile that needs to be set ablaze on a regular basis. I have noticed that the only fire that completely consumes the entire pile, scares me! If I am able to control the fire, it usually does not burn everything up and just causes a lot of irritating smoke!

The Spirit's fire must burn hot and strong so that we are

completely consumed and purified. Revival is the church on fire! We will all feel a bit uncomfortable and a bit out of control when we are baptized in fire. Nevertheless, Our job is to fan into flame the gifts of God upon our lives.

The Holy Spirit is like a fire and a wind. Jesus taught Nicodemus that:

The wind blows wherever it pleases. You hear its sound, but you cannot tell where it comes from or where it is going. So it is with everyone born of the Spirit. (John 3:8)

Consider how weather patterns are literally poured out into an area like water being poured into a basin. When two weather fronts collide, there is usually thunder and lightning before the atmosphere changes. Once the atmosphere is poured out, the entire region is changed. Warm weather replaces frigid air, or vice versa, and life adjusts accordingly.

I believe that the Holy Spirit is poured out over an area in the same way. Literally the Spirit of God comes into a region and shifts the entire atmosphere.

A few years ago, Youth with a Mission gathered dozens of local churches together in our region for a city wide evangelistic outreach. After months of prayer, planning and raising support, the day finally arrived when teams from all over the world came to our city to minister the gospel. The weather on that day was like no other. An abrupt windstorm blew into our region, toppling trees with tornado strength force. It seemed as though the physical shift preceded the spiritual.

That week, Youth with a Mission, working alongside local

churches, saw hundreds of salvations. New believers were added to the body of Christ in large numbers. When the Spirit is poured out in an area, the kingdom of God is released to earth, impacting our communities. God has given me a deep desire for this vision. In fact, the vision statement in our local fellowship is to *change the atmosphere of our city*.

For I will pour water on the thirsty land, and streams on the dry ground; I will pour out my Spirit on your offspring, and my blessing on your descendants. (Isaiah 44:3)

Movement and activity are always associated when the Spirit is present. I think the Spirit should be seen as a verb instead of a noun. Wherever the Holy Spirit is, there is a flow, a movement, or a stirring. The Spirit of God hovered over the waters until God spoke.

Now the earth was formless and empty, darkness was over the surface of the deep, and the Spirit of God was hovering over the waters. And God said, "Let there be light," and there was light. (Genesis 1:2-3)

We should operate in the same manner. When we feel the Spirit of God hovering in a situation, we should ask Jesus what we should declare. As we speak, the Spirit is activated to change the physical realm around us.

Breathing and speaking flow together and give us a picture of how our words carry a 'spirit'. I can remember teaching my children this concept one day. I had them put their hands in front of their mouths as they were speaking. I told them to notice the puffs of air coming out with the words. Words are empowered by breath and carry creative or damaging power within them.

Holy Spirit Flow

The Holy Spirit is compared to streams of living waters. Jesus said:

"Whoever believes in me, as the Scripture has said, streams of living water will flow from within him." By this he meant the Spirit, whom those who believed in him were later to receive. Up to that time the Spirit had not been given, since Jesus had not yet been glorified. (John 7:38-39)

The very nature of water will take the shape of the vessel into which it is poured. In the same way, the Spirit in us takes the shape of who we were meant to be. **"For in him we live and move and have our being."** (Acts 17:28)

Not only do we benefit from His Spirit in our own bodies, the corporate body of the church is filled as well. The Spirit brings us together into one body like liquid Jesus flowing in us and over us. **"For we were all baptized by one Spirit into one body, whether Jews or Greeks, slave or free, and we were all given the one Spirit to drink."** (1 Corinthians 12:13)

Being filled with the Spirit is likened to being filled with wine. When we drink of the Spirit, we become full of the joy of the kingdom. Paul writes to the church in Ephesus: **"Do not get drunk on wine, which leads to debauchery. Instead, be filled with the Spirit..."** (Ephesians 5:18) The disciples experienced drunkenness of the Spirit on the day of Pentecost. The Holy Spirit is like new wine, poured out into the body of

149

Christ, intoxicating us in holy joy! We must drink of the Spirit so that every time the body gathers together, it is Happy Hour!

Joy is an essential ingredient in the kingdom of God, and boldness soon follows. The early disciples were intoxicated before being empowered to witness. We need to be full of the new wine to minister powerfully to the world around us!

New wine is symbolic of joy and represents one third of the kingdom of God. **"For the kingdom of God is ...righteousness, peace and joy in the Holy Spirit."** (Romans 14:17) I often translate joy as fun. I used to take myself too seriously and strived for healings and souls, but had little joy in the process. Now I see more healings and salvations, because I am not trying so hard! I am having fun and the kingdom is coming! I tell people **"Miracles are easy! It's love that is hard!"**

The Lord is the Spirit

I remember hearing a testimony from a skeptic who was visiting a healing revival. After the preacher finished his message, he began to minister to the sick. At that moment, the skeptic recounted in amazement, that he literally saw Jesus stepping into the preacher, like a hand fitting into an empty glove. For the rest of the evening, signs, wonders and miracles began to take place! Would you like Jesus to step into you?

The pattern I find in Scripture is this: the power of the Spirit connects us to Christ, who then connects us to the Father. I believe that the Spirit's role is to connect us to Christ and to one another. In my opinion, viewing the Holy Spirit as "some other person in the Godhead," creates confusion instead of clarity.

A spirit is either holy or unclean; from the kingdom of God, or from the kingdom of darkness. We are breathing in good air or bad air, a good spirit or a bad spirit. I find that too many Christians focus their attention off of Jesus and onto another. As a response to this tendency, I have noticed that there are many popular books urging Christians to place their focus on Jesus. My question is: "How did we ever lose our focus in the first place?" A theological paradigm shift is needed once again in the kingdom!

Paul, in his letter to the Corinthians, says, **"The Lord is the Spirit."** The person of the Spirit is Jesus.
Now the Lord is the Spirit, and where the Spirit of the Lord is, there is freedom. And we, who with unveiled faces all reflect the Lord's glory, are being transformed into his likeness with ever-increasing glory, which comes from the Lord, who is the Spirit. (2 Corinthians 3:17-18)

In summary, let's carefully review the things we have learned: the Spirit of God is our connection to God, and Jesus is whom we walk and talk with every moment of our lives. With Jesus, we approach the Father to bring the kingdom to earth. The Spirit is the breath of life that comes from God the Father, and the Lord Jesus.

When Jesus told us He was sending another, He was not sending some mysterious other person. Jesus is always with us here on earth, simply in another form. He said, **"And surely I am with you always, to the very end of the age."** (Matthew 28:20) As we continue into the next chapter, we will look at the many impersonal aspects of the work of the Holy Spirit.

Reflection

1. Do you feel we should pray to the Holy Spirit? Do you feel we should worship the Holy Spirit? Is it possible we have lost our focus on Jesus by making the Holy Spirit a distinct other person?

2. The definition of spirit is linked to "breath or wind." What does 'breath' signify in a body? If the church is the "body of Christ," how can we breathe easier?

3. Losing connection on our computers or phones is a common occurrence in our lives. How does the Spirit's connection apply to our life in the kingdom?

4. The Bible speaks of people being influenced by an 'evil' or 'unclean' spirit, and those who are in Christ being influenced by the Holy Spirit. How do our actions correlate with what spirit is filling us?

5. How would you like for the person of Jesus to step into your physical body like a hand fitting into a glove? Ask the Lord to step into you right now.

chapter eleven
Jesus Without Skin

*T*here is a new excitement about the Holy Spirit in our day. People are receiving the revelation that God can be felt through the work of the Spirit of God. People are also beginning to experience the gifts of the Spirit with new intensity. We are no longer just nice harmless Christian people, but people who are powerful! As followers of Jesus, we have the same Spirit that raised Him up from the dead!

And if the Spirit of him who raised Jesus from the dead is living in you, he who raised Christ from the dead will also give life to your mortal bodies through his Spirit, who lives in you. (Romans 8:11)

Most of us have probably been taught that the Spirit is a distinct person other than Jesus and the Father. The church has focused on the Spirit as a person, but has often ignored and

153

neglected the many impersonal aspects of the Holy Spirit. I believe we should treat the Spirit of God as 'Jesus without Skin'.

Just as the Spirit connects us to God, the same Spirit also connects us to one another. In our modern world today, we now have devices that allow us to communicate to one another wherever we are. We can be on the other side of the world, yet be looking at each other and talking to one another. In the same way, the Holy Spirit makes our connection with Jesus and the Father close and personal.

By viewing the Holy Spirit as another person, we can be distracted from walking with Jesus. I think we need to embrace the Holy Spirit as our Jesus Connection instead of placing some other mediator between God and us. Jesus alone is the mediator.

Every Body Needs a Spirit

The need for the Spirit of God has never been greater. The world is dying because they cannot breathe. It is breath that brings life! Without the Spirit we are just a bunch of corpses!

One Saturday morning, a friend of mine had our men's group do an exercise. He asked everyone to hold their breath. Then he directed us to perform some common acts of kindness: smile, pray for someone, say something nice, etc. At first we could do a few of these things, but soon we were only concerned with one thing: getting air into our lungs! We were unable to accomplish anything else until we could breathe.

This exercise reminded us of how we must be completely dependent on the Spirit in our service to God. We are paralyzed to do anything until we learn how to breathe! We must inhale *and* exhale to stay strong in the LORD.

When the Lord Himself walked this earth, He modeled how we should interact with the Father and how we should minister. From the very beginning of the ministry of Jesus, **"...the Holy Spirit descended on him in bodily form like a dove."** (Luke 3:22)

Remember, the Spirit was here on the earth while Jesus was ministering. The Holy Spirit is the Spirit of God, the Spirit of Christ, or the Spirit. Many of us have had in our minds that there is a person called 'Holy Spirit', instead of seeing the Spirit as the power, the love, and the connecting force of the kingdom of God.

Never do we see Jesus talking to the Holy Spirit, praying to the Holy Spirit or worshipping the Holy Spirit. Jesus taught us that we worship the Father and stay full of joy through the Holy Spirit.

This is a shift in our paradigm regarding the Holy Spirit for many of us, but one that I suggest we ponder. When the Holy Spirit was 'added to the Godhead' in the centuries that followed the apostolic writings, I sense the message was complicated. The personification of the Spirit requires us to see God as a 'Trinity.' But the simple message of the kingdom is and always has been that **"God so loved the world that He sent His One and Only Son..."** (John 3:16).   Heaven's dynasty is the Son rising up to the throne to advance the kingdom of His Father on earth.   Adding another person called 'Holy Spirit' to the 'Godhead' complicates my interaction to the Father.   Jesus without Skin is 'who' I feel in me and with me on a daily basis!

155

The Holy Spirit Not Included

A straight forward reading of the New Testament shows us that every greeting in the New Testament clearly emphasizes 'God our Father and the Lord Jesus Christ'. There is no other greeting found: no greeting given by the Holy Spirit. If the Holy Spirit was 'another person of the Godhead', why was He ignored? Consider the following greetings found in the letters of Paul and Peter.

To all in Rome who are loved by God and called to be saints: Grace and peace to you from God our Father and from the Lord Jesus Christ. (Romans 1:7)

Grace and peace to you from God our Father and the Lord Jesus Christ. (1 Corinthians 1:32; Corinthians 1:2; Galatians 1:3; Ephesians 1:2; Philippians 1:2; Philemon 1:3)

We always thank God, the Father of our Lord Jesus Christ, when we pray for you. (Colossians 1:3)

Paul, Silas and Timothy, To the church of the Thessalonians in God the Father and the Lord Jesus Christ: Grace and peace to you. (1 Thessalonians 1:1)

To Timothy my true son in the faith: Grace, mercy and peace from God the Father and Christ Jesus our Lord. (1 Timothy 1:2)

To Timothy, my dear son: Grace, mercy and peace from God the Father and Christ Jesus our Lord. (2 Timothy 1:2)

Praise be to the God and Father of our Lord Jesus Christ!
(1 Peter 1:3)

If the Holy Spirit was a person in the 'Godhead,' we should expect mention of Him as well. However there is no such mention! I find it so much simpler to view the Holy Spirit as the breath or wind of God, allowing us to feel the presence of the Father, and His Son Jesus.

As I have pondered this new mindset, I have been reading the word of God through completely new lenses. We need not treat Jesus as distant, but literally here on earth with us! We have every benefit the first disciples had and more! Paul wrote to the Corinthians and said: **"When you are assembled in the name of our Lord Jesus and I am with you in spirit, and the power of our Lord Jesus is present..."** (1 Corinthians 5:4) The Spirit is not the person; Jesus is the person who is present with us! That is why the Lord said, **"For where two or three come together in my name, there am I with them."** (Matthew 18:20)

Holy Spirit Personality Traits

Many of us have been taught about the personality of the Spirit. I am very grateful for the teachings that remind us that we should feel the presence of God and that God is not some impersonal force. I relate to the Spirit of God on earth as the person of Jesus. Therefore, in the scriptures we *should* expect to find personality traits of the Spirit, because Jesus is a person!

The following are the most common texts that point to the Spirit's personality: **"And do not grieve the Holy Spirit of God, with whom you were sealed for the day of**

157

redemption." (Ephesians 4:30)   This verse is central in understanding how God cannot unify a group of believers who live according to their old nature.   Grieving the Spirit is a phrase to help us understand how bitterness and rage destroy the unity in the body of Christ.

Acts 5:3 is also used to define another personality trait of the Spirit. Peter rebuked Ananias for lying to the Spirit.

Then Peter said, "Ananias, how is it that Satan has so filled your heart that you have lied to the Holy Spirit and have kept for yourself some of the money you received for the land?" (Acts 5:3)

When you read a newspaper, you could say, "The newspaper spoke to the situation with clarity and accuracy." No one would think you are crazy by making such a statement. Someone could also say, "The politician lied to the newspaper."   We understand the newspaper did not speak and wasn't lied to- it was the vessel from which information was dispersed. Could it be that the Spirit acts in the same way?

The Spirit is identified as the Spirit of Truth. When truth is taught, the Spirit is present. When error is taught, error is empowered by demonic spirits. Aren't you glad that we have a Father who never lies, but only speaks truth?

But when he, the Spirit of truth, comes, he will guide you into all truth. He will speak only what he hears, and he will tell you what is yet to come. (John 16:13)

We also have the issue of blaspheming the Spirit, which is called the unpardonable sin. The sin of blaspheming means to revile God and things of God.

And so I tell you, every sin and blasphemy will be forgiven men, but the blasphemy against the Spirit will not be forgiven. Anyone who speaks a word against the Son of Man will be forgiven, but anyone who speaks against the Holy Spirit will not be forgiven, either in this age or in the age to come. (Matthew 12:31-32)

Jesus makes this statement in regards to the Pharisees who accuse Him of casting out demons by the power of the devil. I interpret this verse in light of the work of the Spirit in operation. If you condemn the work, you will be unable to respond to the work of the Spirit in your life that is necessary for salvation. (If you are worried that you have committed the unpardonable sin then you haven't committed it!) The mention of blasphemy in these verses does not necessarily signify the Holy Spirit as a person. In context, Jesus seems to refer to blasphemy concerning that which is "of God," not blaspheming of God Himself.

The Spirit Itself?

Most translations use the pronoun 'he' to refer to the Spirit, but there are occasions when the pronoun 'it' is used instead of 'he' in the Greek. Romans 8:18 is an example, as written in the King James Version: **"The Spirit itself beareth witness with our spirit, that we are the children of God."**

If the Spirit is referred to as 'it' even one time in Scripture, in my opinion it calls into question our current theology of defining the Spirit as a distinct other person. The natural flow of Scripture seems to paint the picture of Jesus in another form, close and personal to us. The other paradigm gives the Spirit a role in which I believe is reserved for Jesus Himself. Maybe we have been distracted from placing our attention on Jesus? The personification of the Holy Spirit seemed to be a later addition by theologians to redefine how we relate to God the Father and the Lord Jesus.

Historical evidence tells us that it was not until the later part of the second century that the church began to consider 'a Godhead'. These thoughts later became great sources of division among church leaders. The Roman Empire, after embracing Christianity, sought to resolve the conflict through a series of 'Councils of the Church'. These councils happened seven times over two centuries and produced statements of faith that we refer to as Creeds. Many of the creeds were titled by the person whose thinking prevailed at these councils.

The Athanasian Creed is named after the Bishop of Alexandria, who lived during the fourth century and was highly influential in the theological formation of the Trinity. His views prevailed at the Council of Nicea in 325 AD. The following statement is known as "The Athanasian Creed," named after the Bishop Athanasias. It was written in the sixth century, and it reads as follows:

For there is one Person of the Father, another of the Son, and another of the Holy Spirit. But the Godhead of the Father, of the Son, and of the Holy Spirit, is all one, the glory equal, the majesty co-eternal….. So the Father is God, the Son is God, and the Holy Spirit is God. And yet they are not three gods, but one God. So likewise the Father is Lord, the Son Lord, and the Holy Spirit Lord. And yet not three lords, but one Lord….And in the Trinity none is before or after another, none is greater or less than another, but all three Persons are co-eternal together and co-

equal. So that in all things, as is aforesaid, the Unity of Trinity and the Trinity in Unity is to be worshipped.[1]

The seeds of this statement were planted centuries earlier and developed further as time passed. Theologians felt it necessary to create more intricate language to explain Biblical truths. Though there is truth in this Creed, all truth is not created equal! My observation is the vocabulary used in the Creeds was a distraction from the devotional language of the Bible.

Many scholars recognize the addition of the Holy Spirit as God alongside the Father and the Son, as a new concept, even in the third century. By the sixth century, we see a highly developed theology that was not to be questioned. 'The Athanasian Creed' ended with an 'anathema', which was a condemnation for everyone who did not agree with the Creed in its totality. This controversy resulted in tragic bloodshed. It was the first time in history that Christians killed other Christians over doctrinal differences. The ramifications of this tragedy are with us still today. We should repent for the blood that was shed over this theological controversy! God forgive us!

Who Are We Praying To Anyway?

What we hold as truth should be simple and easy to understand in every culture in the world. Every human being on the planet can relate to the effects a father has upon a child. It is time that we re-emphasize our God as the Father who releases

---

[1] "Trinity." Wikipedia, the Free Encyclopedia. Web. 18 Feb. 2011.
<http://en.wikipedia.org/wiki/Trinity>.

His Son, to be all that He Himself is. 'God as Father' is the message the world needs more than any other message! He sent His only Son so that everyone would believe in Him and have everlasting life. We must fully comprehend the reality of the kingdom that has been conferred upon the Son and is now conferred upon us.

Yet, often when we come into prayer, we become confused about whom we are praying to. Even a child once said, "If Jesus is God, then who is He praying to?"[2] Using terms like 'Godhead' and 'Trinity' make God seem mysterious and foreign. Using language like 'Father' and 'King' give us a clearer model in which to operate in the kingdom.

How are we told to pray? Jesus said in Matthew 6:6, **"But when you pray, go into your room, close the door and pray to your Father, who is unseen. Then your Father, who sees what is done in secret, will reward you."**

The Spirit is called the *paraclete* in John 14:6. Jesus told his disciples, **"And I will ask the Father, and he will give you another Counselor (*paraclete*) to be with you forever—."** The word *paraclete* means to "call to one's side" and is known as "one who consoles, one who intercedes on our behalf, a comforter or an advocate."[3] 1 John 2:1 also calls Jesus a *paraclete*:

---

[2] Ihle, Gerald H. Who Does God Pray To?: Trinity Language Complicates Simple Truth with Study Guide. Pasadena, CA: Hope Pub. House, 2010. Print.
[3] Zodhiates, Spiros, and John R. Kohlenberger. *The Hebrew-Greek Key Study Bible: New International Version*. Chattanooga, TN: AMG Pub., 1996. 1659.

My dear children, I write this to you so that you will not sin. But if anybody does sin, we have one who speaks to the Father in our defense(*paraclete*) —Jesus Christ, the Righteous One.

Many promises we receive in the New Testament point to a close connection between Jesus Himself and the Holy Spirit. He says that He is with two or more who gather in His name. He told His disciples that He would not leave them, but that He would come to them. Listen to what Jesus tells His disciples about the Holy Spirit:

And I will ask the Father, and he will give you another Counselor to be with you forever— the Spirit of truth. The world cannot accept him, because it neither sees him nor knows him. But you know him, for he lives with you and will be in you. I will not leave you as orphans; I will come to you. (John 14:16-18)

Since I have shifted my emphasis of God as Father and Jesus as Son from a traditional Trinitarian view, I have found some room in my theology for the role of the Spirit. Jesus said the Spirit would be given as another, but he also said, **"I will come to you."**

If the Holy Spirit was someone else that was being sent, consider this event in John where Jesus **"breathed on them and said, 'Receive the Holy Spirit.'"** (John 20:22) The disciples were witnessing the person of Jesus after his resurrection, during his forty-day period on earth in His resurrected body. Jesus gave His followers these instructions before He left:

He said to them: "It is not for you to know the times or dates the Father has set by his own authority. But you will receive power when the Holy Spirit comes on you; and you will be my witnesses in Jerusalem, and in all Judea and Samaria, and to the ends of the earth." After he said this, he was taken up before their very eyes, and a cloud hid him from their sight. (Acts 1:7-9)

Ten days later, exactly fifty days after His resurrection, the Holy Spirit was poured out upon the disciples. The disciples experienced an outpouring of the Spirit, because the kingdom of God could now be received by those who called upon the name of Jesus. Peter declared to his fellow Jews:

God has raised this Jesus to life, and we are all witnesses of the fact. Exalted to the right hand of God, he has received from the Father the promised Holy Spirit and has poured out what you now see and hear. (Acts 2:32-34)

Many theologians seem to give the Holy Spirit credit instead of Jesus for what is happening in the world today! The Spirit has been active on earth since the time of creation! The Holy Spirit was flowing through Christ and empowered Him, just as we are to be empowered. **"And the power of the Lord was present for him to heal the sick."** (Luke 5:17)

Jesus and the Father breathe the same Spirit as they release life into the church. The words they speak carry the Spirit into our beings. As we meditate on the words God has spoken, it is as if we are squeezing water out of a sponge. The water we receive from the LORD is life to our souls!

The Spirit of Christ

I find that I relate to Jesus throughout the day by the Spirit, but in times of prayer and seeking God, I go to the Father in the name of Jesus. Paul says that, **"...through him (Jesus) we...have access to the Father by one Spirit."** (Ephesians 2:18)

The Spirit's activity on earth is a picture of Christ Himself walking with us, and us with Him. As we cooperate with him, I sense that we are in training...training for reigning! I think it is Biblical that we keep the presence of Jesus in the forefront of our minds, not as some phantom, ghost, or other personality. Both Paul and Peter refer to the Spirit of God as the Spirit of Christ:

You, however, are controlled not by the sinful nature but by the Spirit, if the Spirit of God lives in you. And if anyone does not have the *Spirit of Christ,* he does not belong to Christ. (Romans 8:9)

Concerning this salvation, the prophets, who spoke of the grace that was to come to you, searched intently and with the greatest care, trying to find out the time and circumstances to which the *Spirit of Christ* in them was pointing when he predicted the sufferings of Christ and the glories that would follow. (1 Peter 1:10-11)

When they came to the border of Mysia, they tried to enter Bithynia, but the *Spirit of Jesus* would not allow them to. (Acts 16:7)

Yes, and I will continue to rejoice, for I know that through your prayers and the help given by the *Spirit of Jesus Christ*, what has happened to me will turn out for my deliverance. (Philippians 1:19)

The Holy Spirit was given to us so that we could be like Jesus. God made us in His image so that we carry within us His Spirit. He did not make us differently, potentially hindering our relationship. He made us **like** Him, so that we can relate to Him.

I am so glad that my children are made in my image. Imagine if they were born a different species? A simple hug or interaction, which is the essence of life, would become difficult! In the same way, God has made us like Him, for the very purpose of relationship. And just like Jesus, we can be a vessel of His Spirit also!

That is why Paul tells us that the hope of glory is "Christ in you!" The Holy Spirit connects us to God the Father and the Lord Jesus Christ in such a way that His presence is felt, and experienced.

To them God has chosen to make known among the Gentiles the glorious riches of this mystery, which is Christ in you, the hope of glory. (Colossians 1:27)

It is my hope that this chapter has given you a perspective of Jesus that will help you continue to walk with Him throughout your day. Jesus will teach you how to be the son or daughter you were meant to be. The Spirit of God is not another person for us to focus on; instead we must seek after the Father and the Son. The Spirit is given without limit- the unending breath of God to those who call on the name of Jesus. **"For the one whom God has sent speaks the words of God, for God gives the Spirit without limit."** (John 3:34)

In the next chapter, I will address a few scriptures that have strongly influenced many of our belief systems. It is my desire to do this in a way that maintains the integrity of the scriptures, yet challenges some of the most commonly accepted translations.

Reflection

1. The Holy Spirit is the Spirit of God, the Spirit of Christ, or the Spirit. As I worship God and His Son, His presence comes and I take a deep breath. How does our breathing relate to our ability to relax? Is your view of God on the throne that He is relaxed?

2. Comment on the statement, "There seems to be a tension between the "unclean spirit" in the kingdom of darkness and the "Holy Spirit in the kingdom of God."

3. Read a few of the following eleven greetings found in the New Testament letters. (1 Corinthians 1:32; Corinthians 1:2; Galatians 1:3; Ephesians 1:2; Philippians 1:2; Philemon 1:3; Colossians 1:3; 1 Thessalonians 1:1; 1 Timothy 1:2; 2 Timothy 1:2; 1 Peter 1:3) There is never a greeting that includes the Holy Spirit. Why?

4. Have you treated Jesus as distant intercessor instead of rejoicing that, as Jesus said in Mathew 18:20, **"…where two or three come together in my name, there am I with them."**

5. The Spirit is sometimes referred to as 'itself' in the New Testament and other times with a masculine pronoun as a 'he.' What conclusions should we come to knowing the Spirit is sometimes referred to as 'it' and

not always as a personal pronoun?

6. Would you consider asking God for forgiveness as part of the body of Christ, for our past sins in shedding the blood of others who disagreed with our doctrines?

chapter twelve
The Integrity of
Scripture

I believe all scripture is inspired in its original writings. I believe everything we need to know is written in the 66 books of the Bible. But I also believe we need to ask questions regarding translations and interpretation. I would say with confidence you can trust what you are reading, but would also point out the possibility of a word or two being changed or modified, whether intentionally or by accident.

I felt this chapter should be added to this writing because of my regard for the integrity of the Scriptures. Our view of the Bible will either ground us in truth, or set us up for deception. Many Christians have had their view of God formed in language not found in God's Word, and now read the

Scriptures with a skewed paradigm. As I mentioned in Chapter Two, our need for Creed has created a mindset that I want to examine.

Most of us have been taught a model of God that has been rooted in a handful of verses. Indeed there are certain verses from scripture that suggest there is reason to keep our current paradigm. The two most prominent scriptures in the New Testament that promote a 'Godhead', are found in 1 John 5:7 and Matthew 28:19.

Which Three Are One?

1 John 5:7, as written in the King James Bible, was taken from a Latin version of the New Testament, instead of an earlier Greek version. This verse is the only time God is mentioned as 'three in one' in the entire Bible.

For there are three that bear record in heaven, the Father, the Word, and the Holy Ghost: and these three are one. (1 John 5:7 King James Version)

This verse has convinced many to see God as "three in one" instead of emphasizing God as Father, and Jesus as Son. Most modern translations remove verse 7 of 1 John 5 and place it as a footnote because of the evidence found in early copies of the New Testament.

Theologically, 1 John 5:7 is the proof text of the New Testament in favor of the Trinitarian view of God. The problem is that this verse lacks credibility as being found in the original text. Looking back at the Council of Nicea in 325 A.D., Dewey M. Beegle points out:

The chief point at issue during the Council was the doctrine of the Trinity. Much of the debate which ensued over this crucial pint has been preserved for us, but nowhere is the Trinity passage of 1 John 5:7-8 quoted as Biblical support for this doctrine. It is impossible that such a wonderful proof text could have gone unnoticed.[1]

How did 1 John 5:7 get into the Bible? Most likely a scribe had written a note on the margins of one of the copies and another scribe "copied this marginal note into the text."[2] Today, few will bring this verse into question because most of us just assume God is 'three in one'.

Almost all new translations, like the NIV, omit the phrase "the Father, the Word and the Holy Ghost," and translate as follows:

For there are three that testify: the Spirit, the water and the blood; and the three are in agreement. We accept man's testimony, but God's testimony is greater because it is the testimony of God, which he has given about his Son. (1 John 5:7-9)

I can understand why the Trinity model was readily accepted because of the mistranslation of this one Scripture. Even many of the modern translations still put in the footnotes the mention of *"there are three that bear record in heaven, the Father, the Word, and the Holy Ghost: and these three are one...".* This obvious insertion has greatly influenced theology.

---

[1] Beegle, Dewey M. *God's Word into English.* New York: Harper, 1960. 19. Print.
[2] Ibid, 20.

Unfortunately, this complicated language has been passed down to us, forcing us to explain how God is 'three in one'. If one chooses complex language to convey the message of God- the Trinity will work. Yet I prefer to keep it simple: God is a Father and Jesus is His Son.

The Matthew Baptism Formula

There is yet another scripture which seems to point to a 'threefold' picture of God, found in Matthew 28:19. The phrase, **"in the name of the Father and of the Son and of the Holy Spirit"** always seemed to me a bit awkward in the text. For many years, I questioned the possibility of whether these words were originally written by Matthew. The scripture is written as follows:

Therefore go and make disciples of all nations, baptizing them in the name of the Father and of the Son and of the Holy Spirit, and teaching them to obey everything I have commanded you. And surely I am with you always, to the very end of the age. (Matthew 28:19-20)

This scripture was first brought to my attention while I was studying Hebrew in Bible School. My professor questioned the authenticity of this verse in its modern translation. He had some reasonable arguments that I decided to put to the test.

First I did a careful study of Acts and discovered there is not even one time the disciples baptized 'in the name of the Father and of the Son and of the Holy Spirit.' In light of these verses being Jesus' final instructions before ascending to heaven, how could the disciples have misunderstood? Either the disciples were directly disobedient to Jesus, or Jesus never used this method of baptism.

The book of Acts reminds us of the simplicity of doing everything 'in the name of Jesus.' Acts 4:12 declares that **"Salvation is found in no one else, for there is no other name under heaven given to men by which we must be saved."** We find that each and every baptism done by the early disciples was in the name of Jesus.

Peter replied, "Repent and be baptized, every one of you, <u>in the name of Jesus Christ</u> for the forgiveness of your sins. And you will receive the gift of the Holy Spirit. (Acts 2:38)

Because the Holy Spirit had not yet come upon any of them; they had simply been baptized <u>into the name of the Lord Jesus.</u> (Acts 8:16)

So he ordered that they be baptized <u>in the name of Jesus Christ</u>. Then they asked Peter to stay with them for a few days. (Acts 10:48)

On hearing this, they were baptized <u>into the name of the Lord Jesus.</u>" (Acts 19:5)

The name of Jesus has all authority in heaven and earth; not the name of Yahweh, or the name the Holy Spirit; but the name of Jesus. Read the book of Acts and discover as I did, that the threefold formula is never mentioned in practice. Even Young's literal translation puts the phrase, "in the name of the Father and the Son and the Holy Spirit" in quotes. Young must have had his doubts about the authenticity of this phrase in Matthew 28:19.

Because of the sacrifice of Jesus and his death, our symbolic death in baptism is made complete. The name of Jesus has all authority in heaven and on earth, therefore we must magnify this name above all others. Romans 6:3-5 tells us that we are **"buried with Him (Jesus) in baptism,"** not with the Father, the Son, and the Holy Spirit. **"For as many of you as have been baptized into Christ have put on Christ."** (Galatians 3:27)

Why would we pray in the name of Jesus, heal in the name of Jesus, cast out demons in the name of Jesus, yet baptize in the name of the Father and the Son and the Holy Spirit? If Jesus commanded his disciples to baptize in the name 'of the Father, and the Son and the Holy Spirit,' why did the early disciples not obey this command?

Many theologians refer to Matthew 28:19-20 as 'The Great Commission'. These last words of Jesus before ascending into heaven have impacted many Christians throughout history. **"Therefore go and make disciples of all nations, baptizing them in the name of the Father and of the Son and of the Holy Spirit...".** (Matthew 28:19)

This first half of 'the Great Commission' was the source of great debate in the early Pentecostal movement as well. A historical movement of the Spirit began in the early 20th century at Asuza Street, near Los Angeles, California. However, a division came in the first decade over a revelation concerning 'the name of the Father and the Son and the Holy Spirit'. The conflict centered around Matthew 28:19 and has yet to be resolved.

In the Pentecostal movement today, we have 'Oneness' Pentecostals or 'Jesus Only' Christians, who claim that Jesus is the Father, the Son and the Spirit. We also have those who stayed 'Trinitarian', such as the Assemblies of God. I believe both views are orthodox because Jesus is treated in the same way the Father is treated. But I also believe both views miss the simplicity of the kingdom!

Paul wrote that, **"...whatsoever ye do in word or deed, do all in the name of the Lord Jesus..."** (Colossians 3:17) Heaven's Dynasty is a message pointing people to God's Son, Jesus, as the One who sits on the throne. He is seated at the right hand of the Father with all authority in heaven and on earth! This is good news! Though the early Pentecostal movement was divided over the issue of baptism, my concern is how we view God.

The Powerful Name of Jesus

There is an underlying principle in Scripture that says, **"Every matter must be established by the testimony of two or three witnesses..."** (2 Corinthians 13:1) Yet reading the parallel verses in other gospels, we do not find the phrase *"the name of the Father and the Son and the Holy Spirit."* Instead we find that we are to operate "in His name"- i.e. referring to Jesus:

He told them, This is what is written: The Christ will suffer and rise from the dead on the third day, and repentance and forgiveness of sins will be preached _in his name_ to all nations, beginning at Jerusalem. You are witnesses of these things. I am going to send you what my Father has promised; but stay in the city until you have been clothed with power from on high. (Luke 24:46-49)

175

He said to them, Go into all the world and preach the good news to all creation. Whoever believes and is baptized will be saved, but whoever does not believe will be condemned. And these signs will accompany those who believe: *In my name* they will drive out demons; they will speak in new tongues; they will pick up snakes with their hands; and when they drink deadly poison, it will not hurt them at all; they will place their hands on sick people, and they will get well. (Mark 16:15-18)

Believers were taught to anoint the sick **"with oil in the name of the Lord."** (James 5:14) The result would be **"that you may be healed."** When two or three gather together **"in His name,"** the result is, that He is there in the midst of them. As the evidence reveals, Jesus commanded us to go and make disciples **"in His name."** As a result, He would be with us **"always, even to the end of the age."**

In contrast to the few key scriptures that infer a 'Godhead' or a 'Trinity', I believe that the weight of Scripture points instead to a simple Father-Son relationship between Jesus and His Father.

The simplicity of this message is powerful. Since the first word out of a child's mouth is usually 'Momma' or 'Dada', why should we attempt to introduce God any differently? Let's introduce God to the world as 'Daddy' and Jesus as Son.

Should some disagree with my conclusions about the translation of these two verses, 1 John 5:8-9 and Matthew 28:19, the emphasis of Heaven's dynasty is still overwhelming in comparison. Our challenge is to embrace the Scriptures in their original writings and to rediscover the message of God the Father and the Lord Jesus Christ. We should always keep our eyes on Jesus alone. If the Holy Spirit is our connection to Jesus, this truly draws us closer to Him, for He is the mediator between God and man. We must not become distracted with anything but Him, and our affections as well, reserved for Him alone.

Reflection

1. Many translations felt it necessary to insure that the "orthodoxy of the Councils" would be found in the Bible. Since the language of 'Trinity' is seemingly not part of the New Testament, should we continue to use it?

2. Does it seem odd that the disciples in the book of Acts baptized "in the name of Jesus," yet Matthew indicates that Jesus instructed them to baptize "in the name of the Father, and of the Son, and of the Holy Spirit?" Could these verses be reconciled?

3. There are thousands of copies of ancient manuscripts of the New Testament. With good accuracy, today's scholars can decipher what was written. How important is this process and how can our "theological bent" get in the way?

4. Why do you feel there is such an emphasis on the name of Jesus throughout the New Testament versus the name of Yahweh?

Chapter 13
The Anointing

Everyone and everything is created and anointed with purpose. The greater the anointing, the greater the ability to accomplish the given task. The anointing is 'a mark or smearing.' This mark signifies the Spirit of sonship upon a person and affirms the realization of who they are in Christ, as well as the recognition of one's purpose and destiny.

The anointing was a sign of consecration or setting apart for a special task or purpose. A priest or king was anointed before being placed into an office or position. When Samuel the prophet found David, he used oil to anoint him as king:

So Samuel took the horn of oil and anointed him in the presence of his brothers, and from that day on the Spirit of the LORD came powerfully upon David. (1 Samuel 16:13)

David knew he was a king. He did not need to be king to be a king. He did not have to wait upon the approval of man to walk in his destiny. On the day Samuel anointed him he became powerful!

Many confuse the anointing and the Spirit. The anointing is not the Spirit per se, but the mark that brings the Holy Spirit upon us. The anointing is the marking of words of destiny on a person's life. The anointing reminds us that we are dearly loved, we bring Him great delight, and we are His, created for glory.

Destiny Codes

Two questions stir in the hearts of mankind: "Who am I" and "Why am I here?" The answer is found in discovering our identity and destiny. In our very DNA, the Father has created us to be a delight and to be like Him in every way. Our DNA is the blueprint within us and stands for "Definitely Not Abandoned!" God has created us to fulfill our purpose!

Our fellowship did a small group study a few months ago to uncover our destiny codes. We began by discovering how God has been programming and wiring our destinies in us even before we knew Christ. We first discovered the meaning of our names. The next week, we talked about life verses or birth verses that have impacted us.[1] Next we encouraged each other

---

[1] A life verse is a scripture that sums up your life that you speak over yourself continually. Mine is Romans 12:11-12, "Never be lacking in zeal but

with God thoughts about one another and also reflected on past prophetic words spoken over us. The final week we encouraged all participants to craft a prayer based upon everything they had discovered about themselves and to pray it daily.

During this time of discovery, I began to pray more effectively over my family. These were not prayers based upon my own wishes. Instead, my prayer was based upon what was already in my family's spiritual DNA. Below is a sample prayer I crafted for my son Nathanael, whose name means, "gift of God."

Thank you Father, for the heart of a king that is found in my son, Nathanael. He is a gift from your heart to this world and carries an impartation of royalty on his life. Nathanael is a man of authority; a young man of great strength who carries a spirit of excellence and overflows in generosity and love. May you multiply abundance to his storehouse that he always may have more than enough. May the heartbeat of heaven be strong in his heart and may he be bold as a lion. He is a giant killer- one who will stand against a tide of evil without feeble hands and knees that give way. He will say to those with fearful hearts, "Be strong and do not fear. Your God will come, He will come with vengeance! With divine retribution, He will come and save you!" Open his heart to receive all the oceans of love reserved for his heart alone. His life will go well because he understands honor. Bless him and the generations that flow out of him forever. May He fulfill his birth verse: Born June 2, 1997. "Honor your father and mother,"

keep your spiritual fervor serving the Lord. Be joyful in hope, patient in affliction a A birth verse is your birth date, let's say June 12, which is chapter 6, verse 12 of any book in the Bible. A few birth verses may be very meaningful and I encourage anyone to seek them out.

which is the first commandment with a promise. (Ephesians 6:11)

Praying crafted prayers according to a person's destiny is a great experience. These words do wonders- especially when the one you are praying for is doing the exact opposite of what you are praying! The crafted prayer will actually prime the pump to release faith and hope. I am so grateful my son Nathanael is modeling these attributes in his life, though he is barely a teenager. Crafting this prayer for him and praying it, keeps me dreaming and meditating on the great things that are ahead for him!

As a father, I also take the opportunity to impart these words at special times to my children. Often I make a fool of myself, choking over the words of affirmation. Though my presentation may be unpolished and I may feel awkward when I release the blessing to my children, I take great pride in my duty to pass on the generational blessing. I encourage all parents to impart blessing to their children, regardless of how they feel.

We cannot give what we have not received. Maybe you need to receive the father's blessing in your own life? You still can, even if your natural father is unable to! Your Heavenly Father is ready and waiting!

During ministry times, I will perform father's blessings over those who need it. I base my blessing upon the story of the prodigal son returning home. Prior to giving the blessing, I ask the person to write down lies that they have believed about themselves. Theses lies are torn up before I place my hand on them. The father's blessing is simply, "The Father loves you and delights in you. He is proud that you are His son/daughter. The Father runs to greet you and welcomes you into his house."

I like to picture a proud father speaking over his son or daughter. As I give the father's blessing, I ask the Lord to share how He feels about the one I am praying. I then ask the Lord to release to them a gift to celebrate the impartation of His blessing. The participant hears the voice of the Father and literally feels the love of God upon them.

After the blessing is given, we throw a party. The father of the prodigal knew the importance of celebration! We shout, we hug, we rejoice because of the goodness of God! You will never fully receive the full revelation of God until you learn how to party.

Anointing of Identity

The Spirit anoints truth and comes upon us when we begin walking in who we are. Jesus began His ministry once He received His Father's blessing. When he heard His Father's words- this was the anointing that marked Him as a candidate for the Spirit of sonship. Isaiah 61:1 says, **"The Spirit of the Sovereign LORD is on me, because the LORD has anointed me."**

The Hebrew word *mashiach* means *'to anoint, smear, consecrate illustrates the idea of anointing something or someone as an act of consecration.*[2] The basic meaning of the word, however, is simply to smear oil or some other substance on an object. Anointing is a picture of a soldier smearing oil on his shield or a painter

---

[2] Zodhiates, Spiros, and John R. Kohlenberger. *The Hebrew-Greek Key Study Bible: New International Version.* Chattanooga, TN: AMG Pub., 1996. 1530.

painting a house. In the Bible, *mashiach* is most often used to indicate 'anointing' in the sense of a setting apart a person for an office or function.

The word *mashiach* is where we get the word Messiah, which is the title given to Jesus. It means *'anointed one, smeared one.'* As is true of the verb, *mashiach* implies an anointing for a special office. The New Testament title of Christ is derived from the Greek *Christos*, which is the exact equivalent to the Hebrew *mashiach*. *Christos* is also rooted in the idea of *'smearing with oil.'* So the term Christ emphasizes the special anointing of Jesus of Nazareth for His role as God's chosen one. *Mashiach* can also be understood, *"..as one singled out or chosen for a task, characteristically one of deliverance..."*[3]. Jesus is the Anointed One; but we also have been 'anointed.'

Christ's followers are called Christians or "anointed ones or smeared ones." Christians are marked by heaven as sons and daughters, destined for greatness and empowered by the Father's blessing. Christians walk in the power and spirit of Sonship.

For you did not receive a spirit that makes you a slave again to fear, but you received the Spirit of son-ship. And by him we cry, "Abba, Father." The Spirit himself testifies with our spirit that we are God's children. (Romans 8:15-16)

---

[3] Ibid. 1530.

We must remember who we are! We can motivate one another by developing a culture of royalty, instead of a culture of shame. The Spirit of son-ship defines who we are and the voice of the Father confirms this reality.

When our ministries focus on sin and what we should *not* be doing, we are more apt to sin and do what we should *not* be doing! If I say, "Do not think about purple elephants," you think about purple elephants, even though I told you not to! In our areas of influence, we should not ignore the negative, but instead, should create a culture of blessing and royalty that can deal with sin in a healthy and effective manner.

The Wound of Fatherlessness

Through my ministry, I have come to realize how deeply the wound of fatherlessness penetrates into the heart of a child. This wound causes fear, insecurity and despair that often leads to mischief and violence in a person's life. The shame of not having a father's love, creates a void that Satan is eager to fill. But the message of the gospel is that we are *not* orphans. We are children adopted into the royal family.

Now if we are children, then we are heirs—heirs of God and co-heirs with Christ, if indeed we share in his sufferings in order that we may also share in his glory. (Romans 8:17)

An heir is 'a person legally entitled to the property or rank of another on that person's death.'[4] So we are heirs of God and

---

[4] Home : Oxford English Dictionary. Web. 16 Feb. 2011. <http://www.oed.com/>.

co-heirs with Christ entitled to the kingdom of God. Heirs contend for their inheritance, but slaves merely follow the rules. Jesus did not come to give us a new set of rules. He came to give us the kingdom.

Most Christians seem to identify with the spirit of fear instead of the spirit of son-ship. We live our lives in fear of breaking the rules instead of in faith advancing the kingdom. John writes:

There is no fear in love. But perfect love drives out fear, because fear has to do with punishment. The one who fears is not made perfect in love. (1 John 4:18)

John had a clear understanding of the power of 'perfect love'. He refers to himself in his writings as **"the disciple whom Jesus loved."** (John 20:21). I too often sign my name as "another disciple whom Jesus loved." I bask in that perfect love. I do not want to be known as someone who loves, as much as I want to be known as someone who is loved! John was not boasting in his love for Jesus but instead in Jesus' perfect love for him! I think John understood that his son-ship was based in love and not in performance or fear.

The anointing brings the power of God upon an individual to complete a task. That is why the anointing is so necessary!! We look to Jesus as our example. We see the Father's blessing released upon Him and then the Holy Spirit also, descends upon Him! This too is our privilege, and under this anointing, our task is to take the planet! *This is a job that only sons and daughters can accomplish!*

Isaiah 61:1-3 describes this experience that each of us should declare:

I can preach good news to the poor.

I can bind up the brokenhearted.

I can proclaim freedom for the captives.

I can release from darkness for the prisoners.

I can proclaim the year of the LORD's favor.

I can proclaim the day of vengeance of our God.

I can comfort all who mourn.

I can provide for those who grieve in Zion.

I can bestow a crown of beauty instead of ashes.

I can bestow on them the oil of gladness instead of mourning.

I can bestow on them a garment of praise instead of a spirit of despair.

The Anointing Bring Light

The anointing also gives us the ability to recognize truth, and will deliver us from fear into trust. It releases us from the spirit of fear and marks us with the spirit of son-ship. When we receive the Father's blessing, we begin to walk in the light of His presence.

As for you, the anointing you received from him remains in you, and you do not need anyone to teach you. But as his anointing teaches you about all things and as that

anointing is real, not counterfeit, just as it has taught you, remain in him. (1 John 2:26-27)

The anointing includes the recognition that we are now part of the family business. God has given us a job to be completed. He is not withholding His kingdom from His children. The Father freely and happily gives it away! **"Do not be afraid, little flock, for your Father has been pleased to give you the kingdom."** (Luke 12:32-33)

When Jesus received his Father's blessing, the devil then questioned him, **"If you are the Son of God..."** The word "if" here is significant. Satan tempted Jesus to question *who* He was. If he could steal His identity, He could control His destiny.

If Satan attacked Jesus at the core of who He is, will he not also attack us with the same strategy? The Father's words of blessing anoint us to accomplish destiny empowered by the Holy Spirit. With this anointing in place, we find courage and boldness for every task given to us. *Without hearing the message, "You are my son, I love you and I am pleased with you," we struggle out of our own lack of identity.*

A few years ago, I was hosting a worship conference at my church. I can remember feeling a sense that something was missing in me, but I couldn't put my finger on it. I sat in the meetings that weekend, where we invited a team from the International House of Prayer of Kansas City. The last day of the conference, I rushed up to the altar after the message and I heard something I had never heard before. The LORD told me, "I am breaking the curse of fatherlessness off your life!" At that moment, I felt something break off me that had been on me a long time. This sense of fatherlessness was literally a curse on me. That day was a new beginning in my journey to walk in my

Father's blessing.

Being involved in charismatic circles for years, I felt there was something out of balance when it came to struggling Christians. We focused more on breaking curses instead of imparting blessing. Recently, my wife and I, and our church family, have become connected with a ministry called Ancient Paths. Founded by Craig Hill, these seminars have helped me realize the importance of opening my heart to the Father's love.

When one feels unworthy, love will be kept at arms-length. The pain of attempting to receive love and potentially losing it, is too much for a heart that is not healthy. Jesus came to heal our hearts and to take away our shame. No matter what we have done, the cross that Jesus hung upon took it all.

Now that I have received the blessing of my Heavenly father, I want to impart it into my sons and daughters. This is not a one- time event, but instead a lifestyle of intentionally blessing those around you. God showed us what we must do as fathers for our sons. We must claim them as our own, "You are my son." We must show them our affection; "I love you." We must let them know we delight in them, "I am pleased with you."

Do You Think Generationally?

The generational blessing that is imparted from Father to Son is the model in which the kingdom is now advancing on earth. We must consider the impact of how we live our lives generationally. In every decision we make, we must ask God for the awareness of how we are affecting the coming generations.

I like the vision of a company called Seventh Generation. They make products that are not only good for the consumer, but also good for the environment. The company derives its name from <u>The Great Law of The Iroquois</u> that states, 'In our every deliberation, we must consider the impact of our decisions on the next seven generations.'[5]

I heard a man speak about a revelation God had given him one day. The Lord told him, as he was praying for his city, to pray "bigger." So he decided to pray for the nation, but God told him "bigger." He then decided to pray for the nations and to his surprise, the Lord told him again, "bigger!" When he heard this, his response was, "How can I pray any bigger?" Then the Lord told him to pray for generations that were yet to exist.

When we look up into a sky full of dark clouds, we realize how clouds impact the atmosphere of our world. Even though the sun shines in all its power and might, the clouds determine how much sun we will receive. On certain cloudy days, it feels as if the sun does not even exist!

In the Bible, clouds represent those who have gone before us. Jesus said in Luke 21:27, that, **"...they will see the Son of Man coming in a cloud with power and great glory."** He is referring to the saints, the great cloud of witnesses, who will be with Him when He comes.

---

[5] "Seventh Generation." *Green Cleaning Products -Diapers -Laundry Detergent -Non Toxic Cleaners.* Web. 16 Feb. 2011. <http://www.seventhgeneration.com/seventh-generation-mission>.

Therefore, since we are surrounded by such a great cloud of witnesses, let us throw off everything that hinders and the sin that so easily entangles, and let us run with perseverance the race marked out for us. (Hebrews 12:1)

The legacy we leave behind will determine how the Son shines on the generations that will follow. The race spoken of in the book of Hebrews is a relay race, and we must run and pass the baton onto the next generation. Get ready to run!

To be effective in establishing a legacy for our future, we should look to repent for the sins of previous generations as well. Interestingly, we find that the ninth chapters of Nehemiah, Daniel and Ezra, all have prayers of repentance for the sins of past generations.

Those of Israelite descent had separated themselves from all foreigners. They stood in their places and confessed their sins and the wickedness of their fathers. (Nehemiah 9:2)

I prayed to the LORD my God and confessed: "O Lord, the great and awesome God, who keeps his covenant of love with all who love him and obey his commands, we have sinned and done wrong. We have been wicked and have rebelled; we have turned away from your commands and laws. We have not listened to your servants the prophets, who spoke in your name to our kings, our princes and our fathers, and to all the people of the land. (Daniel 9:4-6)

Then, at the evening sacrifice, I rose from my self-abasement, with my tunic and cloak torn, and fell on my

knees with my hands spread out to the LORD my God and prayed: "O my God, I am too ashamed and disgraced to lift up my face to you, my God, because our sins are higher than our heads and our guilt has reached to the heavens. From the days of our forefathers until now, our guilt has been great. Because of our sins, we and our kings and our priests have been subjected to the sword and captivity, to pillage and humiliation at the hand of foreign kings, as it is today. (Ezra 9:5-7)

Intercession is the place where we take responsibility for the sins of others. We ask for forgiveness on their behalf by recognizing that our current situation will not change until we deal with our past transgressions.

What was done in the past, has power in the present, and the will continually impact our future. Many respond in shock at the thought of having to take responsibility for someone else's transgression in a previous generation. But thank God for this principle, because it also works for our benefit! What Jesus did for us in the past, now has power in the present, and the results of that action will continually impact us into our future!

Jesus Takes Our Trash

I was driving home a few years ago, and as I came upon my house, I felt my insides turn because I had forgotten to put out my trash the night before! The thought of trying to deal with two weeks of garbage was not pleasant.

Jesus literally came to earth to take our garbage; our perversion, our greed, our lust, our hatred, our homosexuality, our addictions, and on and on I could go. The cross he bore was for my garbage. I don't have to hold on to it any longer, and neither do you. It begins with bringing it out to the side of the road and calling on Jesus for a pickup. One Sunday morning, I literally saw in the Spirit, the Lord walking up and down the aisles looking at the people, pleading with them to give Him their garbage. Jesus is not afraid of it!

All of us deal with garbage in our lives and must have Jesus come for a weekly pick up. It doesn't matter how long you have known the Lord. We need to get the trash out on a regular basis. Why hold on to that which Jesus will freely forgive and take away?

We can't stop here. We must also make Jesus the Lord of our lives. As the Son of God, He is the only one who can forgive sin, and the only way to the Father. The cross cost Him dearly, but He did it to demonstrate how much He loved us. He longed to show us how far He was willing to go, so we might know the heart of the Father.

I encourage you to make Him the Lord of your life today. Jesus will introduce you to the Father. He will give you boldness and confidence, because He is a faithful Son who shows us how to access heaven. Heaven is not just a destination; it's a resource! Through Jesus we can see the goodness of the Lord in the land of the living. We don't have to wait until we die!

You can simply pray, *"Jesus, I believe you died on the cross, rose from the grave, and are seated at the right hand of the Father. I ask you to forgive my sins as I forgive those who have sinned against me. I give you my life and ask that you live in me by your Spirit. I surrender my rights, my life and my future for the sake of the kingdom. I receive the blessing of my Heavenly Father, so that I am now a son/daughter of the Most High God."*

193

I travel out to the International House of Prayer in Kansas City with the brothers on my leadership team just to soak in God and hear His voice. Recently, I felt the Lord instruct me that He was going to take me from "closed" to "close." He showed me the walls in which I had built from past hurts that were keeping Him from being intimate with me. "Closed" was no longer an option. I tell people the sign on our gathering places should say, *"Yes, We Are Open"* instead of *"Sorry, We Are Closed!"*

I urge you to open up your heart and draw close to Jesus. Full surrender means coming unarmed to Jesus, accepting what He did for you on the cross for your sin, and fully receiving all the benefits of His actions. You could never work for, or pay back the offer I am presenting you today. The only action you can take is to open up you heart and let Him in.

From this place of welcoming Jesus into your heart, the journey begins. Every relationship requires time, attention and getting to know one another. Someone once said, "God's language of love is quality time!" You also want to find a place where you can fellowship with other believers. The Spirit of God lives in His body and joining a community of believers, which is called 'the church' is where you will grow. Purchase a Bible that you can easily read and begin to let His Word become your 'ground wire' in life. Ask God the Father and the Lord Jesus to breathe life into you every day as you seek to bring the kingdom of God to earth.

Reflection

1. The word 'Messiah' or 'Christ' is a title given to one singled out, or chosen by God for a task of deliverance. How is the concept of Messiah fulfilled in the person of Jesus?

2. Why did John refer to himself as the **"disciple whom Jesus loved?"**

3. **"Do not be afraid, little flock, for your Father has been pleased to give you the kingdom."** (Luke 12:32-33) Describe your first impression of what it meant to follow Jesus? Did you feel like you were receiving a new set of rules, or a kingdom?

4. *The Great Law of The Iroquois* states, "In our every deliberation, we must consider the impact of our decisions on the next seven generations." Do you ever make decisions this way? How would your decision-making process change with this concept in mind?

5. Take a moment and repent for the sins of past generations. Recognize your connection to those who have gone before you and ask God to give you a heart for those who will follow after you- generations away.

chapter fourteen
Receiving the Blessing

*W*hen we can bring people into the revelation of God as a Father, we will see the hearts of people melt in His love. Unfortunately, most people have had a poor example of this love from their own fathers.

Subtle messages in pop culture reveal the darkness and deep-rooted pain in the heart of this generation. The Star Wars film series was the third-highest-grossing film series of all time. The series incorporates a dark father-son message that echoes in the hearts of many people.

In the Star Wars films, Luke Skywalker faces the emptiness and pain of not knowing his father, only then to discover that his father is his worst enemy, Darth Vader. How many people

197

in our culture today can relate to the pain of Luke Skywalker? The void, emptiness, and shame that accompanies insecure sons, is at the heart of the world's problems.

I believe our greatest message to this generation is in sharing the reality of having a loving Heavenly Father. Jesus came as a Son to show us how to live as sons, how to rule as sons, and how to be loved as sons. Yet our generation is much like Luke Skywalker, living without the revelation of having a Heavenly Father, and the empty feeling of being an unwanted son. (Ladies must be learn to be 'sons of God,' as men must learn to be the 'bride of Christ.")

Not only must we point people to seek the blessing of their father, but we must also encourage it to sink in and take root, so that they too, can be imparters of that same blessing. Contending for the full impartation of the Father's blessing must become our main focus in this life.

The Power of Blessing

God's first act toward man was to bless him. God gave special grace to man by imparting the power of fruitfulness to him through the blessing.

God blessed them and said, "Be fruitful and increase in number and fill the water in the seas, and let the birds increase on the earth." (Genesis 1:22)

The benefits of God's favor are passed on from one generation to another mainly through the father. Since fathers carry this blessing, Satan goes hard after the dad. If Satan can thwart the father, he can thwart or at least hinder the generational blessing from being passed on to the children. The anointing is the Father's blessing imparted to the Son. We must restore this emphasis, beginning in our theology. Every father carries a dynasty within him that needs to be passed on to the next generation.

Blessings need to be spoken in order to be released because words are carriers. They carry the substance of faith or fear. They release destiny, good or bad, because the power of life and death is in the tongue. Jacob, who was renamed Israel, understood the pattern of imparting blessing to the next generation.

He blessed them that day and said, "In your name will Israel pronounce this blessing: 'May God make you like Ephraim and Manasseh.'" So he put Ephraim ahead of Manasseh. (Genesis 48:20)

The LORD imparted into Jacob the ability to be fruitful and multiply, and to see his children become kings of nations. When declarations of blessing are spoken, a prophetic empowerment occurs. Jacob, at the end of his life, imparted blessing, but the story of how he received it must also be told.

Jacobs Steals the Blessing

In the book of Genesis, we find two brothers seeking to secure their father's blessing. Their story begins even while they were in the womb. This is the story about the sons of Isaac and Rebekah.

The babies jostled each other within her, and she said, "Why is this happening to me?" So she went to inquire of

the LORD. The LORD said to her, "Two nations are in your womb, and two peoples from within you will be separated; one people will be stronger than the other, and the older will serve the younger." When the time came for her to give birth, there were twin boys in her womb. The first to come out was red, and his whole body was like a hairy garment; so they named him Esau. After this, his brother came out, with his hand grasping Esau's heel; so he was named Jacob. One son was named Esau and the other was named Jacob. (Genesis 25:22-26)

Esau, according to tradition, was the firstborn and the rightful heir to the blessing. Jacob however, was chosen by God, to receive the blessing of the firstborn. The blessing would allow the firstborn of the family to receive twice as much as the other siblings. For instance, if a man had five sons, the inheritance would be divided into six parts: two parts for the firstborn and one each for the other four. Both of Isaac's boys were positioning themselves for the birthright.

The boys grew up, and Esau became a skillful hunter, a man of the open country, while Jacob was a quiet man, staying among the tents. Isaac, who had a taste for wild game, loved Esau, but Rebekah loved Jacob. Once when Jacob was cooking some stew, Esau came in from the open country, famished. He said to Jacob, "Quick, let me have some of that red stew! I'm famished!" (That is why he was also called Edom. Jacob replied, "First sell me your birthright." "Look, I am about to die," Esau said. "What good is the birthright to me?" But Jacob said, "Swear to me first." So he swore an oath to him, selling his birthright to Jacob. Then Jacob gave Esau some bread and some lentil stew. He ate and drank, and then got up and left. So Esau despised his birthright. (Genesis 25:27-34)

Esau despised or 'made small' the privilege of the birthright just like many people do today. Jewish culture imparted generational blessing and we should revive this practice in the church. Isaac understood his duty as a father to impart the blessing of the firstborn.

When Isaac was old and his eyes were so weak that he could no longer see, he called for Esau his older son and said to him, "My son." "Here I am," he answered. Isaac said, "I am now an old man and don't know the day of my death. Now then, get your weapons—your quiver and bow—and go out to the open country to hunt some wild game for me. Prepare me the kind of tasty food I like and bring it to me to eat, so that I may give you my blessing before I die." (Genesis 27:1-4)

This important moment was to be celebrated with a special meal. Isaac followed in the footsteps of his ancestors, calling the firstborn to receive the blessing. The only problem in this case, was that his wife had received a different word before the twins were born. The LORD spoke to her and said, **"The elder will serve the younger."** Because Isaac refused to listen to the prophetic word given to Rebekah, she became manipulative in her plan.

Now Rebekah was listening as Isaac spoke to his son Esau. When Esau left for the open country to hunt game and bring it back, Rebekah said to her son Jacob, "Look, I overheard your father say to your brother Esau, 'Bring me some game and prepare me some tasty food to eat, so that I may give you my blessing in the presence of the LORD before I die.' Now, my son, listen carefully and do what I tell you: Go out to the flock and bring me two choice young goats, so I can prepare some tasty food for

201

your father, just the way he likes it. Then take it to your father to eat, so that he may give you his blessing before he dies." (Genesis 27:5-10)

Jacob was going to go before his father and pretend to be Esau. He would feel like Esau, smell like Esau and perform like Esau. Yet it was Jacob, the younger brother, in disguise.

He went to his father and said, "My father." "Yes, my son," he answered. "Who is it?" Jacob said to his father, "I am Esau your firstborn. I have done as you told me. Please sit up and eat some of my game so that you may give me your blessing." Isaac asked his son, "How did you find it so quickly, my son?" "The LORD your God gave me success," he replied. Then Isaac said to Jacob, "Come near so I can touch you, my son, to know whether you really are my son Esau or not." Jacob went close to his father Isaac, who touched him and said, "The voice is the voice of Jacob, but the hands are the hands of Esau." He did not recognize him, for his hands were hairy like those of his brother Esau; so he blessed him. "Are you really my son Esau?" he asked. "I am," he replied. Then he said, "My son, bring me some of your game to eat, so that I may give you my blessing." Jacob brought it to him and he ate; and he brought some wine and he drank. Then his father Isaac said to him, "Come here, my son, and kiss me." (Genesis 27:18-26)

Every blessing is sealed with a kiss. Jacob was determined to receive the blessing that his brother Esau deserved. He did this by going before his father clothed as Esau.

So he went to him and kissed him. When Isaac caught the smell of his clothes, he blessed him and said, "Ah, the smell of my son is like the smell of a field that the **LORD** has blessed. **May God give you of heaven's dew and of earth's richness—an abundance of grain and new wine. May nations serve you and peoples bow down to you. Be lord over your brothers, and may the sons of your mother bow down to you. May those who curse you be cursed, those who bless you be blessed."** (Genesis 27:27-29)

This is a picture of what Christ has done for us as our older brother. We can also receive the blessing but only as we come before the Father in Jesus' name. We do not deserve the blessing, but instead receive the blessing that only our elder brother deserves.

Image how awkward and scared Jacob must have been, going before his father, pretending to be Esau. I notice that as believers, we often feel the same way when approaching our Heavenly Father. Jacob went before his father clothed as Esau; we go before our Father clothed in Christ!

Let us then approach the throne of grace with confidence, so that we may receive mercy and find grace to help us in our time of need. (Hebrews 4:16)

The yearning for the blessing never left Jacob's life! On the other hand, we need not strive for our Father's blessing, but must continually strive for its fullness in us. He loves us one hundred percent, one hundred percent of the time. Yet, many only receive ten percent of His love according to how they believe they have measured up. Perhaps they have failed one too many times, therefore ten percent is surely all they deserve. Others believe they are doing pretty well in life, and are able to receive maybe forty or fifty percent of His love. But God's love for us never changes- whether we change or not, seek Him or not; His love never fails.

Jacob needed to be changed to the very core of his identity. Years later he wrestled with God and was transformed.

Then the man said, "Let me go, for it is daybreak." But Jacob replied, "I will not let you go unless you bless me." The man asked him, "What is your name?" "Jacob," he answered. Then the man said, "Your name will no longer be Jacob, but Israel, because you have struggled with God and with men and have overcome." (Genesis 32:26-28)

Jacob's name means, "deceiver, or one who struggles." Even so, he longed for the blessing. He held on until he got the blessing. Our cry must be as well, "I won't let go until you bless me." Once he was given his blessing, he received a name change.

This man, whose name meant 'deceiver', schemed to get ahead all of his life, gets his blessing and becomes a prince! Israel means "prince of God." Our call as well, is to become mature sons and to attain the full measure of the Anointed One.

...so that the body of Christ may be built up until we all reach unity in the faith and in the knowledge of the Son of God and become mature, attaining to the whole measure of the fullness of Christ." (Ephesians 4:11-13)

Our Inheritance in Jesus

Christianity is not behavior modification; it's a nature modification. **"Therefore, if anyone is in Christ, he is a new creation; the old has gone, the new has come!"** (2 Corinthians 5:17) Jesus did not come to modify you, but to kill you! Then, once you are dead, you can experience the power of His resurrection into the royal nature of God.

What Jesus has accomplished through the cross, has now given us rights as sons, just as He is a Son. But you must personally receive Him, because this right only comes through those who enter into to covenant with Him. Jesus offered this covenant to the disciples; a covenant of blood. His blood was necessary because of our sin. Only Jesus' sacrifice is acceptable before the Father for forgiveness. Receive Him and you receive the right to become a child of God. **"Yet to all who received him, to those who believed in his name, he gave the right to become children of God."** (John 1:12)

Heaven is our inheritance, and our rights as sons will be tested by everything hell can throw at us. Our trials and challenges on earth have been modeled by the Son of God Himself. Consider what Jesus faced during His life:

During the days of Jesus' life on earth, he offered up prayers and petitions with loud cries and tears to the one who could save him from death, and he was heard because of his reverent submission. Although he was a son, he learned obedience from what he suffered and, once made perfect, he became the source of eternal salvation for all who obey him. (Hebrews 5:7-9)

205

Obedience to Jesus is not an option in the salvation package. You are either for Him or against Him. There is no middle ground. Today is the day of salvation.

Arise, shine, for your light has come, and the glory of the LORD rises upon you. See, darkness covers the earth and thick darkness is over the peoples, but the LORD rises upon you and his glory appears over you. (Isaiah 60:1-2)

Now is the season for us to arise into our callings, into our inheritance. Jesus was never referred to as a *teknon*, which is the Greek word for "a child."[1] He was always referred to as a *huis*, which in Greek means, "a mature son who would rule his father's inheritance."[2] The title of son can never be taken from Jesus. He was born for it. He always was and always will be 'the Son'. He assumed the title Lord, when He was given all authority in heaven and earth. He will reign until everything is put under His feet. Jesus will rule forever as the righteous Son.

No Longer Slaves

Jesus teaches us how to live, not as favored slaves, but as beloved sons and daughters of the King of the Universe. We must identify with Jesus as a son in order to understand our place at His table. Much of our current theology makes us feel more like slaves, than sons. This is an insult to God Himself. Charles Finney, the great revivalist of the 19th century said in

---

[1] Zodhiates, Spiros, and John R. Kohlenberger. *The Hebrew-Greek Key Study Bible: New International Version.* Chattanooga, TN: AMG Pub., 1996. 1677.
[2] Ibid. 1680-81.

206

his book Revivals in Religion: *"God has no slaves. He does not accept the service of bondmen, who serve Him because they must. He accepts none but a love service."[3]*

As we see the Father delight in his Son Jesus, we can also receive the joy that Jesus Himself experienced. We have inherited the kingdom along with adoption papers as sons and daughters because of Jesus' sacrifice. Now we can follow Christ's example and do what we see our Father doing. No longer do we serve as a slave in fear, but as a son in faith. We become promise motivated, not guilt motivated because we are looking forward to our inheritance. As Jesus said, **"Now a slave has no permanent place in the family, but a son belongs to it forever."** (John 8:35)

Heaven's Dynasty Invading Earth

The discussion found in this book has addressed the first and greatest divide in the history of Christianity. I believe this debate has hindered the clarity found in the relationship of a Father who has raised His Son to His throne. In spite of the arguments, Heaven's dynasty is here now, in Jesus: but is also coming soon its fullness.

The kingdom of God is about a Father and a Son and the lasting dynasty they maintain together. A woman declared over King David, **"..the LORD will certainly make a lasting dynasty for my master, because he fights the LORD's**

---

[3] Finney, Charles Grandison *Revivals of Religion*. Virginia Beach, VA: CBN UP, 1978. 454.

battles" (1 Samuel 25:28). Every king desires his throne to be established through his son and to continue on for generations.

King David reigned as king over Israel for forty years. As he was nearing death, one his sons, Adonijah, decided he would succeed his father. When David heard the news, he took an oath:

As surely as the LORD lives, ...Solomon ...shall be king after me, and he will sit on my throne in my place. (1 Kings 1:29-30)

Solomon was then established as king over Israel and those who did not receive him as king did not live. The throne was secured because God chose Solomon to rule in David's place. At that point in time, Solomon ruled on King David's throne. King Solomon then declared:

And now, as surely as the LORD lives—he who has established me securely on the throne of my father David and has founded a dynasty for me as he promised... (1 Kings 2:24)

The ancients understood the power of a Dynasty. The Son deserved the honor and respect in the same manner as the Father. Anyone who disputed the rights of the son to the throne would not live a long life! Jesus is the Son who has ascended to the throne of His Father.

He who does not honor the Son does not honor the Father, who sent him. "I tell you the truth, whoever hears my word and believes him who sent me has eternal life

and will not be condemned; he has crossed over from death to life." (John 5:23-24)

It is time that Christians emphasize the message of honoring the Son, just as we honor the Father. Jesus is the source of salvation and eternal life. God Himself has released all authority in heaven and on earth to the Son. The throne on which the Father and Son sit, is the dynasty that continues on and will never end.

It is my hope and my prayer that you take what is written in this book and begin reading the Bible with a new perspective. Many have already begun! May the name of Jesus be glorified throughout the earth and may the world bow to Heaven's Dynasty!

Reflection

1. How does the father-son message of the Star Wars saga relate to the pain found in our culture?
2. How does the picture of Jacob seeking his father's blessing give us a picture of how we ought to approach God our Father for our blessing?
3. What does the name Jacob mean? What does the name Israel mean? When did Jacob receive his name change and why did it occur at that moment in his life?
4. Finney said that "God has no slaves." Think of an important figure in American history that owned slaves. How is your view of that person's legacy marred because of their involvement in slavery?
5. Treating Jesus the same way you treat God is necessary in the kingdom. Does the perspective of a dynasty relate that important kingdom message properly?

about
the author

Chris Monaghan and his wife, Debbie, live near Richmond, Indiana, U.S.A. Chris and Debbie are the Senior Leaders of a group of believers in the Richmond area called Gateway Vineyard Fellowship. We focus on changing the atmosphere of our city through worship, teaching and humanitarian acts. Gateway seeks to create a movement centered on revival that flows out of our new identity in Jesus as sons and daughters in the kingdom of God. Chris and Debbie expect supernatural happenings whenever and wherever the body of Christ gathers together and regularly see physical and emotional healings take place. They also serve as coordinators for Family Foundations International and promote the Ancient Paths Seminars in their region. Chris and Debbie have five children: four boys and one girl.

Made in the USA
Columbia, SC
21 July 2019